Prayer

Prayer

A STRATEGY BASED ON THE TEACHING OF JESUS

§

Dr. Bob Beltz

ISBN: 1979874999
ISBN 13: 9781979874991
Library of Congress Control Number: 2017918691
CreateSpace Independent Publishing Platform
North Charleston, South Carolina

to all my friends at
Highline Community Church

Contents

Foreword

§

AMERICANS LOVE "HOW TO" BOOKS. From gardening to stock market speculation, self-help books that teach people how to do something they are interested in, or how to achieve some form of desired success, are always popular. This is such a book. It is filled with good ideas and practical advice on one of the most important subjects of life...prayer. Dr. Bob Beltz offer answers to questions that have perplexed all of us, including, among other things, how to overcome the "internal monologue" that makes it almost impossible for God to speak to us, and how to avoid becoming distracted when praying.

But as you read this book you'll discover that it offers much more than "how to" advice. Bob has written a moving, personal account of his own experiences, including a dramatic encounter with the living God. It is a powerful affirmation that God hears and answers our prayers.

In the pages that follow, Bob demonstrates again and again why he is one of the greatest teachers in America. He has a wonderful gift for making significant theological concepts accessible and relevant to everyday experience. He succeeds in portraying prayer in its rightful context: simple, direct, and incredibly profound.

I believe you will enjoy this book. I know you will be blessed and inspired and perhaps, like me, a bit humbled. But more important, I pray that, as a result of what you are about to read, your prayer life will be greatly enriched.

- William L. Armstrong -
President, Colorado Christian University
Former U.S. Senator

Introduction

§

"HOME IMPROVEMENT" WAS ONE OF my favorite television programs. On the show, comedian Tim Allen played the host of a fictional public television program called "Tool Time." Tim loved his tools! Without tools, simple jobs become impossible. With the right tools, tough jobs often become easy.

Through the years, I have met a multitude of people of faith who struggle in the area of prayer. I also know, being a pastor myself, that most of these men and women have often been encouraged in sermons to place more emphasis on their prayer lives. Most desire to do so. But often, a pastor's exhortation lacks the instruction on how to accomplish this task. The congregation doesn't know where or how to start to see significant change in their experience of prayer. They need a tool.

In 1989, after years of struggle in my own prayer life, I became the object of a special work of grace. God helped me develop a more satisfying and meaningful prayer life. He gave me a strategy that helped put my motivation into action. To help other men and women who struggled in this same area, I began to develop a tool that would help people grow in their experience of prayer. That strategy was first explained in a book I wrote titled *Transforming Your Prayer Life*.

When the publisher of the book went out of business, I was asked to update the original book and target the growing men's movement. The book became part of a spiritual trilogy I authored, and the title was changed to *Becoming a Man of Prayer*.

Now, several years later, that book has gone out of print. As part of a larger goal to keep all my books "evergreen", I have once again updated the book and again attempted to make it accessible to both men and women. After nearly thirty years, I continue to use the tool I've written about in this book. I have attempted to once again balance a theological understanding of prayer with a practical approach to prayer based on the way Jesus taught the disciples to pray. I hope that as you read the book, and put into practice the strategy contained in it, you will experience a renaissance in your own prayer life.

Bob Beltz
Littleton, Colorado
November 7, 2017

PS – Since I have rewritten all the text myself, and don't have an editor to check what I have done, please forgive any errors in spelling, grammar, or punctuation. I tried my best!

CHAPTER 1

Becoming a Man or Woman Who Prays

§

I am a man of prayer,

(PSALM *109:4)*

I'VE HAD A NUMBER OF encounters with God over the last forty-five years that have impacted the course of my life. What I experienced in the Spring of 1992 was the most profound. I was on a small island in the Puget Sound, just across the water from Gig Harbor, Washington, where I had gone to spend twenty-one days in a guided experience of silence and solitude. What happened on that island changed my life. I was touched by God.

I've come to believe that there are two kinds of people in the world who claim to have had such encounters. On the one hand, there are those who are not quite right in the head and in fact have had no encounter with God, however real their experience may seem. On the other are very normal human beings who have had an authentic experience with the living God. I will leave it to you to determine into which category I fall.

It is nearly impossible to describe what happened on that small island. In many ways, it defies description. I had embarked on this spiritual adventure hoping to have an experience with God of "biblical magnitude." I have to confess that in my mind such an experience needed to be either audible or visual. I figured that if you couldn't have a biblical-type of encounter after twenty-one days of solitude, prayer, and total isolation, then such an experience could not be had in our day. What happened to me was not visual. It was not audible either. What I did experience was more profound than either an audible or even a visual experience of God.

The only way to describe what happened on that island is to say that God broke through to the core of my being with His being. I experienced what many of the more mystical Christian writers throughout history have called *union* with God. It happened a number of times during my three weeks on the island and has happened periodically ever since. I made contact with God. Actually, God made contact with me. It was an experience I had desired for years. It was a reality that I am convinced everyone who seeks to know and love God desperately longs for.

Why me? I promise you it was not because of any holiness or advanced spiritualty on my part. I would call myself the "chief of sinners" had not one more worthy than I already taken the title. I am convinced that what happened to me on Fox Island was the culmination of several years of learning to pray in a way that led to this experience with God. I am also convinced that God desires to break through to any man or woman who will properly position themselves to receive such contact. The vehicle designed to facilitate such contact is called *prayer*. In the following pages, I hope to share with you what I have learned and am learning about this wonderful spiritual vehicle.

THE TURNING POINT

It should have become an embarrassment much sooner. How many times had I responded to inquiries concerning my spiritual life with a statement like, "It's going well *but* I really need to work on my prayer life." For almost twenty years I had found time to read and study the Bible. During that same time, I had read a small library of books on the subject of Christian spirituality, had completed both a master's degree and a doctorate in pastoral theology, and had been working full-time in vocational ministry. Yet my prayer life was not what I knew it should be.

Don't get me wrong. My life was not without prayer. I always spent some daily time in prayer and went through periods of more intensive prayer as well. I had even spent half-days and whole days in prayer. But I had never been able to develop a consistent, effective, satisfying discipline of prayer. Too often, I felt like prayer was a one-way communication. I knew God was there, but I rarely felt his presence.

As I struggled with this area of my relationship with God, it became apparent to me that I was not alone. The usual response to my confession of inadequacy in this area was an emphatic "Me too!" Many men and women struggle to have a consistent discipline of prayer in which they not only believe God is engaged in the process with them, but in which they experience his presence and have the sense that in a very real way they are making contact with the divine.

In a *Life Magazine* article entitled "Why We Pray" (that came out during the time I was wrestling with this issue), researchers indicated that an incredible percentage of Americans pray regularly. Ironically, as many as ten percent of those who report that they don't believe in God still pray - just in case. What the article failed to say is that most of these prayers have little to do with the core purpose of prayer. Prayer is intended to be a vehicle for fellowship and communion with God. But, over fifty-five percent of those responding to the research reported that they pray less than five minutes each day. Not much time for fellowship and communion!

What prayer has become for most men and women is a quick plea for a bit of divine intervention in the need of the moment. Surprisingly, the secular person in the workplace and the religious man or woman who occupies the pew on Sunday often have the same problem. They don't know *how* to pray in a way that brings them into the experiential presence of God and leads to His intervention in their lives and the needs of the world. I know. I was one of them.

In what appears otherwise to be a bleak picture there is actually good news. We live in a time when many men and women hunger for a life of more consistent and meaningful prayer. I know. I am one of them.

A Personal Pilgrimage

I have discovered at this point in my life that I usually end up doing those things I am highly motivated to do. I know that as a follower of Christ, the Bible's instructions and exhortations in the area of prayer should provide sufficient motivation to pray. Whatever caliber of prayer life I maintained over the years has been motivated by such obedience. But there is a problem with the quality of prayer generated by the motivation of obedience alone. But knowing our hearts, God has other ways to motivate us if he sees sufficient willingness and desire lying dormant within.

Because I have many friends who know of my interest in things of the spirit, I am regularly given books that someone assures me I have to read. My schedule and limited supply of physical, spiritual, and emotional energy keep me from reading many of these books. Because of this dilemma, I consider it a work of grace that I did read Frank Peretti's *This Present Darkness.*

At the time of my struggle, the book was a best seller. The novel is about the reality of the unseen universe and how it constantly affects that part of reality that we sense and experience. At one level, the plot of the book describes events taking place in the fictional town of Ashton. Troubling things are happening in town. The moral and ethical atmosphere of the community is in a state of decline. The small college located in Ashton is being infiltrated by professors who advocate strange metaphysical beliefs and practices. In short, numerous unhealthy dynamics are at work in the community.

While the primary plot is developing along these lines, a second level of plot is introduced. This plot line is taking place in the realm of the unseen. A spiritual conflict is raging over Ashton. The genius of the book lies in Peretti's ability to portray the reality of the unseen spiritual realm and how it impacts what is taking place in Ashton. The angelic host of heaven is engaged in battle against the spiritual forces of evil. The temporal events taking place in the lives of the citizens of Ashton are by-products of this war raging in the spiritual realm.

The most important message of the book lies in the fact that the outcome of the battle in the heavenly realm is significantly influenced by what is taking place at a little church in the town. A small group of Christian men and women begin to pray for their town. As these men and women pray, the host of heaven prevail over the forces of evil. But when they fail to pray, the battle turns in favor of the forces of evil.

As I read the book, one thought kept hitting home. I was repeatedly reminded of how prayer is intended to be effectual in influencing heavenly realities. In turn, those heavenly realities impact earthly situations. This truth began to rekindle a strong desire to see my prayer life transformed. I had the motivation. Now I needed a strategy to turn that motivation into action.

I began to study the way Jesus taught the disciples to pray. The critical moment in my study came as I was looking at Matthew 26:36-46. This is the text where Jesus goes into the Garden of Gethsemane to pray the night before he is crucified. He pulled his three closest disciples aside and asked them to keep an eye out while he prayed. You know the scenario. Jesus prayed; the disciples slept. When Jesus discovered that they were asleep, He asked this question: "Could you not keep watch with me for *one* hour?"

I began to have the uneasy feeling that if my present experience of prayer were to continue, Jesus might ask me the same question someday. I had been "sleeping".

That day I made an important decision. I decided to wake up! I resolved that by the grace of God, and with the help of the Holy Spirit, I would work to change my prayer life. I decided to learn to pray the way Jesus taught his disciples to pray. I meant it, and I did something about it. I linked my motivation to a commitment. Then, I added action to that commitment.

The phrase "one hour" from Jesus' question hit home. Could I begin to pray for one hour a day? I decided I needed to take "baby steps" so I prayed and asked God to specifically help me pray for fifteen minutes. In the next chapter I will show you how I used the Lord's Prayer during each of my sessions as I worked to increase my prayer experience. I prayed exactly fifteen minutes that day.

The next day I prayed and asked God to help me pray for a half hour. Again, I began to use the strategy I will teach you. I prayed for exactly thirty minutes! The next day I asked for help praying forty-five minutes. I further developed the tool we will learn and when I felt like I was finished praying, I looked at my watch. I had prayed for forty-five minutes. Finally, four days into my new commitment, I prayed for one hour. During that time, I repeatedly experienced God's presence in a fresh way.

That day marked the beginning of an exciting journey. I began to experience a more significant and meaningful prayer life. I didn't always pray for an hour, or even an extended period of time. But, I can tell you this; the prayer dimension of my relationship with God began to be transformed. That was over twenty-five years ago! What I learned then is just as valuable to me today as it was when I first started my journey.

Let me ask you a very important question. How is *your* prayer life? If it is satisfying, effective, fulfilling, and productive, you probably don't need to read this book. Give it to a friend. But if you are struggling in this area of your spiritual life, if you are not spending time with God in prayer and experiencing him in a way that is filling the hunger of your heart, then this book is for you! As you read these chapters and work through the seven assignments, I believe your prayer life - and your relationship with God - will be transformed. It will require a decision and a commitment on your part. Are you ready to do what it takes? Then let me challenge you right now to make the following commitment:

Father, by your grace and with your help, I resolve this _____day of _____to do whatever it takes to experience a transformation in my prayer life.

Signed: _____

CHAPTER 2

The Need for a Strategy

§

Lord, teach us to pray,

(LUKE 11:1)

As I STRUGGLED WITH MY prayer life, I realized I needed someone who knew about prayer to teach me. I discovered I was not alone. I was in good company. Twelve men who spent three years with Jesus had the same need. One day, these men came to Jesus and asked him to teach them to pray, (Luke 11:1).

This was an interesting request in light of its historical context. I am sure that by the time the disciples made this request they had spent quite a bit of time and energy attempting to pray. They were all Jewish men who had prayed since their youth. Is it possible they were feeling as frustrated as you and I in their efforts to pray? I am convinced that in the year they had spent with Jesus up to that point, they came to recognize that he provided a model that challenged all their previous assumptions about prayer.

Jesus was always praying. They would wake up in the morning and he was gone. Where? He had risen before dawn and gone off to pray, (Mark 1:35). At other times, he prayed all night, (Luke

6:12). Sometimes he sent the disciples on to their next destination while he remained behind to pray, (Matthew 14:23). Nearly every critical event in the life and ministry of Jesus Christ was preceded by times of extended prayer. One day as Jesus was praying "in a certain place" the disciples had seen enough. "Teach us to pray," they asked, (Luke 11:10).

A STRATEGY

In response to their request, Jesus taught the twelve a pattern of prayer we call the Lord's Prayer. It might be more accurate to call it "the disciples' prayer". It was given to them by Jesus to make their prayer life more productive and effective.

Biblical scholars hold two distinct opinions as to the intention of this prayer. Some believe it was given as a *form* prayer to be used liturgically and repetitively. Those who hold such a view claim that the use of liturgical prayer was common among the rabbis of Jesus' day.

Others believe that the prayer was intended to be a *pattern*, or *outline* that provided the disciples with topics about which to pray. Those who believe this was the intention of Jesus' instruction also claim that the use of a pattern prayer was common among the rabbis of Jesus' day. They also point to the passage in Matthew's gospel where the Lord's Prayer is preceded by a warning against the vain, repetitive prayers of the "pagans", (Matthew 6:7).

Both uses of the prayer have proven valid throughout the history of the church. In my life, the pattern approach became the strategy I needed to see significant change in my prayer life. I had the motivation. The motivation was even linked with a commitment. I was ready to take action. But I lacked a strategy to make my motivated, commitment-based action effective. Using the Lord's Prayer as a pattern provided such a strategy.

For many men and women, this is the missing ingredient that can make their prayer lives more relevant and exciting. Few men and women question that prayer is one of the most important dynamics of spiritual life. We are convinced. We are motivated. We are even committed. But we don't know *how* or *what* to pray. Once we see how to develop each component of the Lord's Prayer into a dimension of our prayer time, we'll have the strategy needed to experience a relevant and exciting prayer life.

As a common man's theologian, I love teaching through the life of Christ. During such teaching I have often analyzed the components of the Lord's Prayer. Unfortunately, having analyzed, I failed to adequately incorporate these components into my own prayer life. That has changed. I have developed and integrated each of the areas Jesus addressed into my times of prayer.

The Lord's Prayer can be found in two places in the New Testament; in the Sermon on the Mount in Matthew, chapter six, and in Luke, chapter eleven. If you put these texts together you will find that the pattern Jesus gave the disciples has seven components. The prayer, thus constructed, looks like this:

1. *Our Father in heaven,* (Matthew 6:9; Luke 11:2).
2. *Hallowed be your name,* (Matthew 6:9; Luke 11:2).
3. *Your kingdom come, your will be done, on earth as it is in heaven,* (Luke 11:2; Matthew 6:10)
4. *Give us this day our daily bread,* (Matthew 6:11; Luke 11:3).
5. *Forgive us our sins* (debts), *for we also forgive everyone who sins against us,* (Matthew 6:12; Luke 11:4).

6. *Lead us not into temptation, but deliver us from evil,* (Matthew 6:13; Luke 11:4).
7. *For yours is the kingdom and the power and the glory forever. Amen,* (Matthew 6:13).

Isn't it amazing that these are the very words given by Jesus to twelve men like you and me? If you take each phrase of the prayer and categorize the intention of the instruction, you have a brief outline of the sevenfold strategy it provides. In the following chapters I will attempt to develop each of these components in a way that will give you an idea of how to incorporate it into your own prayer time. For now, let me give you a brief overview:

1. *"Father"* - Prayer begins with a conscious act of seeking to enter into the presence of God. I call this component "Getting started".
2. *"Hallowed be your name"* - Having entered into the presence of God in prayer, Jesus instructs us to direct our attention to God himself. This component becomes a time I call "Getting focused."
3. *"Your kingdom come"* - As a third component of prayer, Jesus extends the invitation to appropriate his intervention in our lives and the needs of the world. In light of this, our third area will be called "Experiencing divine intervention."
4. *"Give us this day"* - It is not until this fourth component is reached that our focus shifts from God's agenda to ours. "Praying for provision" becomes the time we pray about our own needs.
5. *"Forgive us our sins"* - Under the category "Experiencing forgiveness" we will learn to utilize the resources made

available by the finished work of Christ to keep our lives in line with God's moral imperatives.

6. ***"Deliver us"*** - I've labeled the sixth component "Developing spiritual protection." During this part of your prayer time you will build a spiritual defense system around your life and family.

7. ***"Yours is the kingdom, and the power, and the glory"*** - The seventh and final component of the strategy is a closing time of theological affirmation. Having moved through all the dimensions of the pattern, it is appropriate to bring our time of prayer to a close with the declaration that God is the King and his is the kingdom. This will be a time to address some final issues.

These seven components form the framework of a working strategy designed to help us become more effective in our prayer lives. In one short lesson Jesus taught the disciples an incredibly effective and thorough pattern of prayer. What I hope to accomplish in the coming chapters is to help you develop each of these components into a more comprehensive strategy to turn your experience of prayer into an exciting adventure.

TAKING ACTION

Learning *about* prayer is important. But learning *to* pray requires action. Throughout this book I will attempt to teach you a great deal about prayer. I also hope to be your spiritual coach and give you helpful assignments to put into practice what you learn. Here comes your first assignment.

For the next week, I am going to ask you to pray for only five minutes a day. You can pray longer if you want, but the assignment is only five minutes. These five minutes are going to be guided by the seven components in this chapter.

I also want to introduce you to two tools that will help you immensely as you learn to pray. The first is the Bible. When I work out physically I always need a little time to warm up. I find that I have the same need when I pray. My favorite time to pray is in the morning. I get out of bed, get a cup of coffee, and head for the spot I have set aside to spend time alone with God. I open my Bible and read a short passage to get my mind focused on spiritual things.

I find reading a psalm to be a great way to warm up. I usually also add a chapter from some other book of the Bible. For your first five days, read Luke 11:1-13 daily, and Psalms 1-5, one psalm a day.

The second tool that this book is designed to help you develop is a personal prayer notebook. This notebook will become your guide as you pray. It is designed to help remind you of the components you will be developing. You will find that along with being a great reminder, it will also help you overcome what is one of the greatest problems most people have when praying - distraction. I use composition notebooks for this purpose. I now have dozens of them I've used over the years and periodically I go back and see what I was praying about and what I felt like God was saying to me.

To begin with, you can use the pages I have included in Appendix B. I have already numbered seven blank pages with Roman numerals I through VII. I have also labeled each of the pages with the corresponding phrase of the Lord's Prayer and its title. As you move through this book, you will fill in those pages with your own outline to help you pray. In Appendix A I have given you a model to help.

For the next five minutes slowly pray though each of the seven phrases of the Lord's Prayer. Think about what each phrase means. If something comes to mind as you reflect on the phrase, turn it into a topic of prayer. As an example, if as you pray "Give us this day our daily bread" you realize that you need help with some financial issue, ask God to help. Be specific.

By the time you have finished this book, these pages will be filled with new ideas and items you want and need to pray about regularly.

ASSIGNMENT ONE:

1. Read Luke 11:1-13 daily.
2. Read one psalm daily. (I often read the psalm that corresponds to the date. If you divide the book of Psalms into thirty day periods you will have five cycles of psalms that correspond to the date.)
3. Review the commitment you made at the end of chapter one.
4. Reflect on the seven components of the Lord's Prayer in your prayer notebook.
5. Using your outline, pray five minutes daily!

CHAPTER 3

Getting Started

§

When you pray, say: "Father...",

(LUKE 11:2)

I AM A DAD. I'VE been one now for over thirty-five years. When I wrote the first edition of this book, I was a rookie. I have found being a dad to be one of the most challenging jobs in the world. Few do it well. I am constantly aware of how my performance as a dad has impacted the emotional, physical, and spiritual well-being of my children. For most of these thirty-five plus years I have felt that I have done an inadequate job, regardless of how much time I invested in my role as a father. Most of my male friends who have children feel the same way.

Part of the reason I am so aware of my performance as a father is undoubtedly rooted in the emotional void in my own life created by the lack of a stable, loving, and nurturing relationship with my own father. I don't have many conscious memories of my early childhood. What memories I do have of my father are mixed. I remember some good times - playing catch in the yard and learning how to throw a football and catch a baseball. In later years, I remember him showing up to watch me compete in sports.

I also still have some painful memories. I remember the day my mom and dad decided to end their marriage. I remember going to live with my grandparents. After an attempt at reconciliation, I remember dad leaving for good. I never had a normal relationship with him after that.

I remember the morning my sister called and told me that dad had died suddenly of a heart attack. There was shock and tears and the sense I had lost forever something I never really had.

The need for a caring, nurturing father is foundational for emotional and spiritual development. I see this clearly now that I have been a father. Children need a dad who is there for them. They need a dad who cares and nurtures. Their "love tanks" need to be filled daily. They need a dad they can count on.

I believe there is a child in each of us who still has the same needs. The truth is that our need for a father can never be fully met by a human father. To one degree or another, all earthly fathers will let us down and disappoint. Most families have some degree of dysfunction. But there is a relationship designed to meet this deep need.

We have been created to relate to God as our heavenly father. He is a *perfect* father. He is always present and available. He is loving, caring, and nurturing. He is committed to meeting our physical, emotional, and spiritual needs. No time in our day is more important that the time we spend with him.

As I began to use the Lord's Prayer as a pattern, the fatherhood of God became more of a reality in my life. I realized that even though I confessed and affirmed that God was my father through Christ, I had very little experience of this in my life. I've talked with many other men and women about this issue and find this to be a common dilemma. Many of us need a vehicle whereby the theological truth of the fatherhood of God can become real in our experience. This is why it is so significant that the first component of our strategy grows from Jesus' teaching that we should begin prayer by addressing God as "Father." Authentic prayer is an expression of a father-child relationship.

"Father"

For many of us, addressing God as father seems normal. Most of us were taught to pray this way since childhood, even if our families were not very religious. This was not the case in Jesus' day. A quick trip through the great prayers of the Old Testament will reveal that even the most holy men of the old covenant did not address their prayers to God as "Father."

There are some incredibly powerful and moving prayers in the Old Testament. Many of the psalms are beautiful prayers of King David. Sometimes David prayed, "O God." Sometimes it was "O Lord." At times of special intimacy, he prayed "O *my* God," or "O *my* Lord." But nowhere will you find David addressing the living God as "Father."

Daniel was also a man of prayer. His prayer life was so powerful that the angel Gabriel was sent to respond personally to Daniel's great prayer recorded in Daniel, chapter nine. Yet he did not address God as "Father."

The patriarchs, the prophets, and the priests of Israel were all men of prayer. But they never addressed their prayers to God as "Father." That privilege is uniquely ours because of who Jesus is and what he has done on our behalf. Through his death and resurrection, Jesus gave believers the right to become children of God. Because of this truth, he instructed the disciples to begin to pray with a focus on God as father.

By beginning our prayer time this way, we start praying within the framework of a father-child relationship. Our initial thoughts are on God, our heavenly father, and on our relationship with him. I think of this as a time of getting properly positioned before God. For me, this involves working through several factors.

EMPOWERMENT

In Romans, chapter eight, the Apostle Paul tells us that we don't know how to pray like we should. I heartily affirm this truth! Authentic prayer, in which genuine communication takes place, is a gift of grace. Paul goes on to explain that part of the ministry of the Holy Spirit is to help us in this area, (Romans 8:26-27). I find it immensely helpful to acknowledge this inability and to ask for the promised help of the Holy Spirit. I might begin by praying something like this:

> *Father, I would like to spend some time today with you. You know that I don't have the ability to pray in a way this is pleasing to you and significant for me. Therefore, I ask the Holy Spirit to help me pray as the Bible promises.*

God will answer this prayer. I cannot emphasize strongly enough how important this step is in the process of developing a significant life of prayer. Apart from God's enabling, I do not have the ability to pray in a way that feels authentic.

I also use this period of positioning to pray about the quality of my prayer time. I have a tendency to become distracted when I pray. Sometimes my attempts at prayer have seemed ineffective and even boring. You might have experienced the same problems. If so, it is appropriate to ask the Helper something like this:

*Holy Spirit, help keep me from being distracted as I pray. Make
this a time filled with a sense of reality.*

Remember, the Bible tells us that we do not have because have not
asked, (James 4:2). Most of us have never thought about praying
about praying. This preliminary part of our prayer time sets the
stage for what follows.

RELATIONSHIP

Having asked for the helping ministry of the Holy Spirit, it is now
time to focus our thoughts on our *relationship* with God. Prayer is
primarily a vehicle of relationship. I am reminded of this as I think
about the words used in the Bible to express this relationship.

Two important New Testament words teach us about the
unique relationship we have with the living God through Jesus
Christ. In both the Matthew and Luke accounts of the Lord's
Prayer, Jesus taught the disciples to address God as *Pater*. This
is the word usually translated as "father". But Jesus not only addressed God as *Pater*. Occasionally, he would use the word *Abba*.
This was an Aramaic term of endearment that might best be translated "Daddy." The Bible tells us that the presence of the Holy
Spirit in our lives is a spirit of adoption. By adoption we receive
our spiritual birthright to also call out to God as *Abba*, (Romans
8:16; Galatians 4:6).

I am the father of two tremendous human beings. When I
first started developing this approach to prayer they were both
young children. I will always be their father, but in those early
days I loved being their "daddy." Now I'm just plain old Dad.

When my son was young, he had been diagnosed as having
delayed speech development due to loss of hearing. After using

a few words early, he just quit talking. We were quite concerned until he spoke again at the age of two-and-a-half. My wife had taken him to see the launch of a number of hot air balloons. I had been out of town, and when I returned I walked in the door, looking forward to seeing both my wife and kids. When Baker saw me he said, "Fire makes the balloons go up." Not bad first words for a delayed kid! His mother had not told him this. He had figured it out all on his own.

One morning not too long after this incident I was up early to finish preparing for a bible study I was teaching that morning. Baker woke early and came out of his bedroom to find me sitting on the sofa reviewing my notes. He climbed up next to me on the couch. Suddenly, it was like a light bulb went on in his mind. He looked up at me with a big smile, put his index finger on my arm, and declared, "Baker's Daddy!" At that moment, he could have asked me for anything and I would have given it to him! I was thrilled by this simple recognition and affirmation. It was a tremendous example to me of how God feels about us. He delights when we come to him and call him "Abba"..."Father"..."Daddy".

When we direct our attention toward God, and call him Father, we consciously enter his presence. Theologically speaking, we are always in God's presence. But through this approach to prayer we are able to experientially and consciously enter that presence. We are set to spend time in fellowship and relationship with our heavenly "Daddy." This is what I mean by *spiritual positioning*. It sets the tone for all that follows.

Know this: you have a father in heaven who is perfect, loving, interested, involved, gentle, present, available, concerned, wise, caring, and good. He delights in your desire to spend time with him. In light of this truth you might continue to pray something like this:

Father, I pray that I might experience your presence today. Help me live in a father-child relationship with you. Help me experience your love for me. Help me experience you today as my Abba, my heavenly Daddy.

This relationship, not only affirmed but experienced, is critical to a healthy and vital prayer life. As you pray with this component in mind, slowly but surely you will begin to sense the loving touch of God on your life. Prayer is the vehicle that bridges the gap between what I know in my head and what I experience in my life.

AUTHENTIC ENCOUNTER

I had been praying this way for about two years when I took my spiritual journey to Fox Island. This was a guided time of silence and solitude that required me to commit to twenty-one days of guided isolation. I was not allowed to have a phone, books, magazines, radio, computer, or TV. I was not allowed to work out. I was put into a situation where all distractions were removed to give God space to work me over! He did.

The first week of my time on the island I was aware of how much noise I normally experience in my daily life. Once the external noise was removed, I became even more aware of the inner "noise" that goes on inside our minds. It is hard for God to break through and communicate when the noise and distraction of life in the modern world, both internal and external, is so loud and constant. If we are going to hear God, we will need to take extreme measures.

By the end of the first week, I had quieted down in a way I had never experienced before. Early in my second week, I was reflecting on the origins of the word *Abba*. I could almost picture a small

Aramaic child calling out for his father, *"Abba...Abba..."*. Suddenly, *Abba* was no longer simply a theological concept, but the cry of a young child for their father.

As I reflected on this, I began to experience a shift in my conceptual framework. I imagined someone holding me. It was Jesus. He was there. Then came the first breakthrough. No longer was I imagining this scene. In an unexplainable way, I was experiencing it. I *was* being held by God, and he penetrated all the filters that kept me from experiencing his real presence. At the depths of my being I was having an experience of the touch of his being. It was overwhelming. By far, it was the most powerful experience of the presence of God I had ever had.

This encounter was repeated a number of times in the days that followed. On rare occasions, I have experienced it since. It was something I had longed to have for more than twenty years. It was real contact and connection with God. It couldn't have happened had I not started to pray the way Jesus taught, and particularly by positioning myself in prayer in the father-child relationship.

Now it is time for you to seek contact with your heavenly father. Go to the first page of your notebook (Appendix B) that is numbered with Roman Numeral "I" and titled "Getting Started." Using an outline format divide your page into two sections. Label the first half "A." Next to the letter write "Empowerment". Under this title put your Arabic number "1." Write "My powerlessness" after the number. Spend a moment telling God that you don't have the ability to pray like you want to. Then put down your number "2." After this number, write "His power." Ask God to give you the ability to pray today. You might make a note to yourself reminding you that Romans, chapter eight, gives biblical support to what you have just prayed. In my own prayer notebook, I have biblical support noted for every idea I am going to give you in this book.

Go about half-way down the page and put a capital "B." After this letter write the word "Relationship." Carefully go through the assignment below, writing in your notebook specific issues to pray about in order to get yourself properly positioned in your relationship with the Lord.

With our inner lives properly positioned, and having entered into our Father's presence to spend time with him, we are now ready to get our hearts and minds focused on God's agenda in prayer. The next section of the strategy will help us accomplish this task. But first, make sure you do your assignment. See if you can increase the time you pray to ten minutes, five days, this week.

Assignment Two:

1. Read a psalm every day. Read Ephesians 1:1-13; Romans 8:12-17; and Galatians 4:1-7.
2. Go to the "Getting Started" page in Appendix B and develop this page of your notebook.
3. Ask God to help you pray daily. Shoot for ten minutes a day.
4. Pray through this first component:
   a. Ask for help in staying focused.
   b. Reflect on your relationship with God as Father.
   c. Pray for more reality in your father-child relationship with God.
   d. Ask the Holy Spirit to take control of your life today.
5. Pray briefly through the other components of the pattern using the pages in Appendix B.

CHAPTER 4

Getting Focused

§

For you have exalted above all things
your name and your word,

(Psalm 138:2)

Prayer requires focus. The second component of the strategy helps develop it. It helps us get our hearts and minds on God's agenda. Jesus taught the disciples that when they prayed they should pray, "Hallowed be your name." Attempting to understand and implement this instruction will bring our prayer experience into sharper focus.

The Name

In the culture of Jesus' day, a name carried great significance. A name was intended to be a reflection of a man or woman's character. Parents gave great thought to the names they gave their children. Often, when God had a powerful encounter with an individual, he would change that person's name to reflect the change in character produced by the encounter. The most well-known case of this was Jesus changing Simon's name to Cephas. We translate "Cephas" as "Peter". The name meant "rock".

God's name is a revelation of his nature and character. To *hallow* means to treat with great reverence. It requires contemplation of God's person and attributes. Focusing our thoughts this way will help lead to a response the Bible calls *worship.*

As I began to develop this dimension of prayer, I had several important insights. I was immediately aware of how little of my previous prayer experience was focused on God. I know that sounds strange, but think about it. Most of us use prayer as a time to ask God for what we need or want him to do. That is a part of prayer, but it is not the primary purpose of prayer. I was neglecting a critically important dimension of prayer. I needed to fix my attention on God and who he is in order to know how to pray about my needs. In the words of Jesus, I needed to "seek *first* his kingdom and his righteousness" (Matthew 6:33) to get my mind in tune with God's Spirit. To accomplish this objective, I implemented a simple plan to use God's name in prayer.

If you have taken a course in improving interpersonal relationships you've probably been told how important it is to remember people's names. When people remember my name, it communicates to me that they have invested a certain amount of caring energy into cultivating a more significant relationship with me. Names are important. Do you know the name of God? The word *god* is not a name - it is a title. Most people use the title as if it was a name, but it isn't. In the Bible, God makes his name known and repeatedly expands this revelation.

The book of Exodus contains the story of Moses. In Exodus, chapter three, we read how God called Moses to go back to Egypt to liberate the people of Israel. Moses responded to this call by asking God a very important question: "Who shall I say sent me?" (see Exodus 3:13). Moses was asking God to tell him his name. God answered Moses question: "Tell them I AM has sent you," (Exodus 3:14). In the Hebrew text God's name is written using four consonants. What we translate "I AM" can be transliterated out of Hebrew by using the letters YHWH. *YHWH* is the name of God. If you add vowels to the consonants the name would be *Yahweh*. Many times, in the Old Testament, the vowels from the Hebrew world *Adonai*, which means *Lord*, were added to these consonants and the word *Jehovah* became one of the names of God.

What does this name tell us about God's nature? *YHWH* is a form of the Hebrew verb translated "to be." It can be translated several different ways. It communicates that *YHWH* is the God who is. He exists. He has always existed. It also is an expression that can have a causative sense. When understood this way, it would be translated as "I cause to be." One final possibility is to translate this name as expressing the thought "I will be who I will be." This expresses his sovereign control of the universe and our individual lives. Thinking about God in this way begins to get my focus on him.

The Names

As you move through the Old Testament, following the revelation of God's name in Exodus, chapter three, God reveals more of his nature by adding descriptive words to the name *YHWH*. Each of these compound names reveals something more of God's nature, and provides a great resource for focusing our minds on God.

In my prayer notebook, I have entitled the second section "Getting Focused." The first subsection is devoted to focusing my thoughts on the name of God. I use this time to express my gratitude that my heavenly father is the sovereign, omnipotent, and benevolent God of the universe. These truths capture the significance of his name.

The second subsection contains seven sections, each devoted to one of the compound names of God found in the Old Testament. I pray through each of these names by reflecting on their significance in my life and then thanking God for each of these characteristics of his love for me. To help you gain an appreciation for these names, let me give you a brief introduction to the God who is:

YHWH-tsidkenu (Jeremiah 23:6)

Two of these compound names relate to God's redemptive activities in human history. *YHWH-tsidkenu* means "The Lord our righteousness." This name reminds us of God's gift of salvation in Christ. Usually at this point in prayer I remember that Jesus' name in Hebrew was *Ya'shua.* This name means "God is salvation." I thank God that when I had no righteousness of my own and was in a desperate situation of need, Jesus Christ died for me. He is now the source of my righteousness. There is a very real sense in which Jesus is the fulfillment of the name *YHWH-tsidkenu*, (I Corinthians 1:30). I pause and think about what Christ has done for me. His atoning death and resurrection are the basis on which all of life takes on meaning and significance. I thank God for this gift.

As I pray and reflect, I will often have a thought come to mind that is related to what I'm praying about. When that happens, I always write the thought in my notebook. This is often how God speaks to us. I periodically go back through these notes and am amazed how they have a sense of some message God is trying to say to me.

YHWH-m'kaddesh (Exodus 31:13; Leviticus 20:7-8)

Not only is the Lord the source of my righteousness, he is also "the Lord who sanctifies." That is the meaning of the name

YHWH-m'kaddesh. In conjunction with declaring me right in his eyes because of Jesus, God is also at work in my life to change me and make me, in my character and experience, more the person he created me to be. Reflecting on this name triggers my memory about how desperately I need the Holy Spirit to work in my life each day.

I am eternally grateful for God's gift of forgiveness. I am confident that the death of Christ was fully adequate to pay the price for the forgiveness of my sin. My forgiveness, and God's declaration of my rightness in relationship to him, is finished business. But in my day-to-day life I need help. I need to be changed. I am painfully aware that I am powerless over the results of my previous separation from God. Apart from his intervention, my life is unmanageable and unfruitful. Gratefully, as I think about the significance of God's name being *YHWH-m'kaddesh*, I acknowledge that he is at work *in* me to restore sanity and productivity.

YHWH-shamma (Ezekiel 48:35)

Having focused on God's transforming work in my life, I am reminded that the agent who makes my personal transformation possible is the Holy Spirit. All that the Father purposed, and the Son provided, is made real in my experience by the ministry of the Holy Spirit. Because of the ministry of the Holy Spirit, God is "the Lord who is present."

The most sacred piece of turf in the land of Israel has always been the top of Mt. Zion where the Temple of the Lord stood. The real importance of the Temple was not found in what people did there. The unique characteristic of the Temple was found in the fact that God had chosen to manifest a tangible expression of his presence there. Although the infinite God cannot be contained in a building made by human hands, in love he gave his people a visible manifestation of himself in the innermost room of the Temple. This room was called "the Holy of Holies." There, over the Ark of the Covenant, God's presence was revealed in a visible way. The Israelites called this manifestation the *Shekinah*, a Hebrew word meaning "residence." Where the *shekinah* was present, God had taken up residence.

God no longer makes his presence known in a building made of stone. His great desire since the dawn of creation had been to dwell in the lives of men and women who live in a loving relationship with him. Because of the indwelling presence of the Holy Spirit, the Bible tells us that our bodies have now become the temple of the living God, (I Corinthians 3:16; 6:19). Jesus is our Immanuel - God *with* us. He is present. As I pray, I thank him that he is present by the Holy Spirit and ask the Spirit to influence every fiber of my being with that presence. Jesus promises that he is with us always, (Matthew 28:20), and that he will never leave or forsake the one who belongs to him, (Hebrews 13:5). He is *with* me and *in* me because he is *YHWH-shamma*.

YHWH-rohi (Psalm 23:1)

Classics are usually classics because they are so...well, classic! That is certainly true of Psalm 23. How many of us have read, memorized, quoted, and reflected on this psalm without ever realizing that the opening declaration of David is one of God's names? *YHWH-rohi* is translated in most English bibles by the phrase "the Lord is my shepherd." In the Hebrew text, the phrase is a single word. God relates to his children as a shepherd to his flock. A shepherd guides his flock; God desires to guide us. A shepherd provides for his flock; God is willing to provide for us. A shepherd protects his flock; God protects us. A shepherd is the source of security for his flock; God can be such for you and me. In the

New Testament Jesus tells us that he is the Good Shepherd, (John 10:10).

As you think about this name of God, pause and give thanks for each of these characteristics of a shepherd. Pray that this day the Lord would shepherd you by guiding, providing for, and protecting you. He is your shepherd. Praise and thank him that he is *YHWH-rohi*.

YHWH-jireh (Genesis 22:14)

One of the great revelations of the nature of God is found in the life of the patriarch Abraham. Having waited until the ripe old age of ninety-nine to have a son who would fulfill God's promise, Abraham must have thought it was crazy that God could actually want him to sacrifice Isaac.

As Abraham and Isaac trooped up Mount Moriah, Isaac must have been a bit suspicious. He asked his dad an obvious question: "The fire and the wood are here, but where is the lamb for the burnt offering?" (Genesis 22:7).

You probably know the story. God saw Abraham's willingness to sacrifice his only son. We can assume that this was what God was really looking for. God provided a ram caught by its horns in a thicket for the sacrifice. In response to this divine intervention and provision, Abraham named the place *YHWH-jireh*. The name means "the Lord will provide." Our heavenly father is a provider. He meets our needs. His name reveals his nature. He promises his provision. This promise finds its fulfillment in the work of Christ and his providential care over our lives. As Paul wrote to the Philippians, "my God will meet all your needs according to his glorious riches in Christ Jesus," (Philippians 4:19).

Not only is God a provider, he is a *good* provider. James wrote that every good and perfect gift comes from his hand, (James

1:17). The psalmist said that "no good thing does he withhold from those who walk uprightly." Thinking about, and reflecting on this name of God should move us to thank him for his provision and faithfulness in our lives. He is *YHWH-jireh*.

YHWH-rophe (Exodus 15:26)

God is a healer as well as a provider. As the nation of Israel was coming out of their bondage in Egypt, God made a wonderful promise. They had crossed the Red Sea and traveled three days into the Desert of Shur. The people were desperately in need of water, but could find none. They came to a place called Marah where there was water, but it was "bitter". This means it was unfit for human consumption. God used Moses to perform a miracle of healing of these waters to make them "sweet", meaning they were now healthy. God then used this event to teach them a new dimension of his nature. He promised the people that if they lived in obedience (which they failed to do), he would keep them from being afflicted with the diseases of Egypt. Then he spoke his name: *YHWH-rophe*, a name meaning "The Lord who heals you."

I have to confess that the area of supernatural healing is a complicated one that I don't fully understand. I have been blessed to have experienced repeated instances in the life of my family when I have seen God's healing nature expressed in response to prayer. In my times of prayer, I thank God and praise him for those experiences. I am extremely grateful that God is *YHWH-rophe*.

YHWH-nissi (Exodus 17:15)

This name of God was given to an altar Moses built after the Israelites defeated the Amalekites during the time of their exodus, (Exodus 17:15). *YHWH-nissi* means "the Lord is my banner." The significance of the name lies in the recognition that

God is the source of victory and success in our lives. He is there to help us fight the battles we face. When he becomes the source of our salvation, sanctification, security, provision, protection, guidance, and healing, we no longer need to fear. He has broken the curse of the Law and the sources that create our fear of failure. He has promised us hope and a bright future, (Jeremiah 29:11). He shows us how to live a life of spiritual prosperity and success, (Joshua 1:8). Our lives will not be free of difficulty, but every difficulty can become an opportunity to experience his intervention and the victory that only he can give. He is *YHWH-nissi*.

YHWH-shalom (Judges 6:24)

As you focus on the names of God in prayer you will find your mind flooded with thoughts about the particular dimension of God's nature you are focused on. Often these insights are part of an answer to prayer. You asked the Holy Spirit to make your prayer time real and meaningful. Now he is interacting with your mind and giving insights as you pray. Feel free to stop and meditate on these thoughts. I have had days when it took over an hour just to pray through these eight names of God.

The final name is something of a summary name. *YHWH-shalom* means "the Lord is peace." Most of us remember the story of Gideon because of his famous fleece experiment with God. We often fail to remember that Gideon had a powerful encounter with the Angel of the Lord prior to this. In response to this encounter, Gideon, grateful that he encountered God and lived, built an altar. He gave this altar the name *YHWH-shalom*, (Judges 6:24).

Gideon was used in this instance to reveal a profound truth: "the Lord is peace." The Hebrew word *shalom* is a much more comprehensive term than our English word *peace*. It encompasses the concept of well-being, which is a by-product of a proper relationship with God. In the Old Testament, the shalom of God was intimately related to the blessing of God. The great liturgical blessing of God given to the Levites in the book of Numbers demonstrates this relationship:

> *The Lord bless you;*
> *The Lord make his face shine upon you*
> *and be gracious to you;*
> *The Lord turn his face toward you*
> *and give you peace (shalom),*

(Numbers 6:24-26).

The blessing of God brings the peace of God. If you have entered into a relationship with God through Jesus Christ, he is the ultimate source of your peace, (Ephesians 2:14). Peace is the result of God's Spirit working in your life and bearing spiritual fruit, (Galatians 5:22). As you pray, ask for the peace of God in your life. Focus on this dimension of God's nature, remembering that your well-being and wholeness come from Him. Thank him that he is the God of peace: *YHWH-shalom.*

THROUGH THE GATE AND INTO THE COURT
Focusing on God - hallowing his name - can become an incredible source of joy and peace in our lives. This is the missing ingredient in prayer for many men and women. As we fix our thoughts on who God is, we will often find ourselves experiencing a desire to respond by giving God praise. This is worship. Heartfelt worship is intended to be foundational to the prayer experience. The psalms were written as songs of praise and worship. Each is a

tangible expression of the psalmist's prayer life. As I began to focus on God, and worship him in my times of prayer, I experienced a shift in my sense of awareness. I began to experience the presence of God.

This should not have surprised me. Psalm 100 instructs us to "enter his gates with thanksgiving and his courts with praise," (Ps. 100:4). As we spend time focusing on God's attributes and character, we should begin to experience his presence. Our focus and response bring us spiritually "through the gates" and "into the courts" of heaven. Prayer becomes joyful and exciting because "in your (God's) presence is fullness of joy", (Psalm 16:11). This focus in prayer helps move us into the experience of God's reality.

Focus is a vital part of an effective prayer life. Something happens in our hearts and minds as we spend time concentrating on who God is. If you put energy into this early part of your prayer time you will find that prayer becomes vital and exciting. You will have consciously entered God's gates with thanksgiving and his courts with praise. Having moved into his presence and sharpened your spiritual focus, you will be spiritually prepared to take on the next component of prayer. You will be ready to place many of the critical areas of your life under his will and to ask for his divine intervention.

As you work on this week's assignment, try to get your prayer time up to fifteen minutes.

Assignment Three:

1. Reaffirm your commitment to pray.
2. Ask the Holy Spirit to help you pray five days this week.

3. Develop the "Getting Focused" section in your prayer notebook:
   a. Make *YHWH* the "A" of this part of this section.
   b. Review the meaning of "*YHWH*" from this chapter and make note of anything that strikes you to pray about.
   c. Under "B", outline the eight *YHWH* names of God.
   d. Jot down what each name means to you.
4. Pray:
   a. Pray through your positioning issues from the last chapter.
   b. Pray through the *YHWH* names of God.
   c. Remember to give praise and thanksgiving for each name and what it represents.
   d. Briefly pray through the rest of your outline from the Lord's Prayer.
   e. Read Psalm 100 daily.

CHAPTER 5
Experiencing Divine Intervention, Part One

§

Call to me and I will answer you,

(Jeremiah 33:3)

One fact is certain these days: We could all use a little divine intervention in our lives! Prayer makes such intervention possible. Jesus instructed the disciples to pray for the kingdom of God to come and the will of God to be done "on earth as it is in heaven." Authentic prayer brings heavenly realities to bear on earthly situations. I'll explain what I mean in this chapter and the next.

Understanding the Kingdom
To fully appreciate and apply this component of prayer, we need a proper understanding of the Kingdom of God. The concept of the Kingdom permeated Jesus' life and teaching. From the beginning of his ministry, when he declared "Repent, for the Kingdom of God is at hand" (see Mark 1:15), until his ascension

when the disciples asked, "Is it at this time that you will restore the Kingdom to Israel?" (see Acts 1:6), Christ's ministry was all about the Kingdom.

In the New Testament, the word *kingdom* is used to translate the Greek word *basileia*. This word is used in two different, yet important ways. Often the word refers to the *realm* of a king. When you and I think of the concept of a kingdom we usually think of it this way. For Western thinkers, "kingdom" usually speaks of geography. We assume that if there is no geographical land mass over which a king reigns, there is no kingdom. To many people in Israel during Jesus' time, the concept of the kingdom was primarily connected to a military Messiah who would overthrow the Roman oppressor and reestablish a political kingdom over the same geographical area King David once ruled.

In biblical times, this same Greek word (*basileia*) was also used without reference to a geographical realm. In these cases, the word emphasized the "reign" or "dominion" of a king without the necessity of a geographical realm. In this sense, the kingdom exists wherever the king reigns, whether over a chunk of nearly barren land in the Middle East, or in the heart of a man or woman walking down the street in New York City.

When Jesus taught that "the kingdom of God is within you" (Luke 17:21), he was using the word to indicate reign or dominion. It was in this context that Christ challenged his followers to "seek first the kingdom of God, and his righteousness" (Matthew 6:33). He was not instructing them to go on a search for an elusive piece of real estate. He was encouraging them to seek the rule and reign of God in their hearts as their highest priority. When they sought, and achieved this objective, they would experience the inner reality of the kingdom. God's priorities would then dominate and dictate the agenda of their lives.

God ultimately reigns over the entire universe. But for the moment there appears to be one piece of turf in the cosmos that is not operating under his reign. You guessed it...a small, insignificant planet in the western spiral arm of the Milky Way galaxy, populated by (among other organisms) a peculiar carbon-based life form called "humans". Following certain events that transpired in what is often referred to as primeval history, the dominion over this piece of real estate was forfeited to a character who himself had rejected the reign of God sometime before the dawn of time as we know it.

You and I have the fortune (or misfortune) of living on what C. S. Lewis called "the silent planet". One day what Jesus Christ has already accomplished through his atoning death and triumphant resurrection will be fully consummated. On that day, the kingdom of this world will once again be "the kingdom of our Lord and of his Christ, and he will reign for ever and ever" (Revelation 11:15). Until that day comes, we have been given an incredible opportunity. Through the vehicle of prayer, we have been invited to appropriate unseen kingdom realities - the power of God intervening and impacting earthly affairs - for the purpose of bringing them to bear on earthly situations. Prayer enables us to ask for direct divine intervention.

THEN AND NOW

Along with our understanding of the *reign* versus *realm* emphasis of the kingdom concept, we also need to understand something of the kingdom's timing. There is a definite futuristic or eschatological dimension to this prayer concerning the coming of the kingdom. For years, I believed that the significance of praying for the kingdom to come involved the second coming of Christ and the fulfillment of Revelation 11:15. Certainly, that is one dimension of what Jesus was teaching. But we live in a unique period of history where it is possible to experience what some theologians call "the presence of the future".

Through Jesus Christ the kingdom of God has made a "secret" invasion of human history. In the Old Testament, the people of God understood history in a relatively simplistic, linear fashion. They knew that their time and history had been seriously warped by humanity's distorted relationship with God and the consequences of the Fall. They also knew that a time of incredible upheaval was coming in the future when God would overthrow the current regime and establish his kingdom. This transition period was referred to as the Day of the Lord. Following this upheaval, the kingdom of God would be firmly established in the age to come.

Jesus changed our understanding of these things. At a pivotal point in his ministry, Jesus was casting out demonic spirits from people whose lives were under the controlling influence of these evil beings. Rather than being ecstatically happy about this, some members of the religious establishment accused Jesus of casting out demons by the power of a demonic character named Beelzebub, another name of the devil.

Jesus' response went straight to the point. If Satan were casting out Satan, he would be destroying himself. This made no sense. He went on to announce (see Matthew 12:26-28), that if in fact he was casting out demons by the power of God (which he was), then the kingdom of God had come upon them (which it had). The future had arrived. Heavenly realities were coming to bear on earthly situations. There was a presence of the future in the present. There was a measure of fulfillment without complete consummation.

What does all this have to do with our prayer lives? Everything! There is an exciting, present application of the prayer "your kingdom come."

The Kingdom and Prayer

We live in a time when the presence of the future is a constant possibility. We have been given the amazing privilege to pray that God will intervene and influence earthly affairs. Jesus taught us to pray for the coming of his kingdom and for the will of God to be done on earth as it is in heaven. In the grammatical structure of the Greek text, there is a degree of urgency and entreaty that borders on a sense of command in this instruction. There is a *now-ness* to the prayer. When we pray this prayer, we are calling on God to intervene in our lives and in our world.

Note that we come to this point in our time of prayer only after an extended period of spiritual focus where our hearts and minds have been set on God, himself. Even as we shift from a heavenly focus to the initial stage of what we might call intercession, we are still concentrating of God's agenda. Our prayer remains focused on his kingdom and his will. This time of prayer begins with a spirit of relinquishment. We are saying to the Father, "Not my will but yours. Not my kingdom first; your kingdom first!" This spirit of relinquishment is then followed by an authoritative entreaty.

When we pray for God to influence earthly situations through his kingdom realities, we should expect that this will happen. Jesus didn't instruct the disciples to pray this way without the expectation that their prayers would release his power on earth. Let me illustrate.

In Acts 12, we learn that Peter was arrested and thrown into prison. Since Herod Agrippa had just put James, the brother of John, to death, we might assume that Peter was in serious trouble. We are told that in response to Peter's predicament "the church was earnestly praying to God for him" (Acts 12:5). What do you think they were praying? I don't believe they were asking God to help Peter accept his circumstances. I don't even think they were praying for God to comfort Peter in his hour of need. I don't believe they were praying for Peter to accept his imminent departure from the land of the living. I believe they were praying for *divine intervention*. They wanted to see the power of heaven brought to bear on Peter's earthly circumstances!

We are also told *how* they were praying. "The church was *earnestly* praying...for him" (Acts 12:5). It appears that with a degree of appropriate authority they were praying that God's kingdom would come on Peter's imprisonment. Perhaps they believed it was not God's will for Peter to die yet. If so, they were praying for Peter's deliverance. The results were exciting.

Blatant divine intervention took place. God answered the prayers of the church. He sent an angel who woke up Peter (without waking up the guards he was chained to), unlocked the chains that bound him (still without waking the guards), and led Peter right out of the prison. Peter and the angel walked by the guards, who were apparently blinded, and out of the iron gate of the city (which opened by itself). Peter was free! Heavenly realities had come to bear on earthly circumstances in direct response to the prayers of God's people. This was not a Hollywood special effect. This was real. The event was so extraordinary that not even Peter believed it was actually occurring. The text tells us that he thought he was having a vision (Acts 12:9).

Peter then went to the house where the men and women of the church were praying. They were still praying for him while Peter stood at the door knocking. When the servant girl reported that Peter was at the door, their response was classic. "You are out of your mind, they told her" (Acts 12:15). They didn't believe that God had actually done what they had prayed for! I'm afraid that I can relate too often. Meanwhile, Peter was still knocking. Finally, they opened the door. The text says they were "astonished". I believe that is one of those great biblical understatements. Maybe the lights finally went on. "Wait a minute! Peter gets jailed, we pray, God springs him! God answers prayer!" God's kingdom had come and his will had just been done! I have a feeling the prayer life of everyone involved in this episode took on a whole new vitality.

Here is the point. Jesus gives those who bear his name the privilege of appropriating divine intervention through prayer. Don't get me wrong - we do not change God's will. It is not our kingdom we are praying for. We affirm the will of God through prayer and bring the reality of his kingdom into our lives. What an exciting privilege! I hope you capture a sense of the incomprehensible opportunity that God has placed at our fingertips, which awaits our appropriation and application.

With these facts firmly established, let's look at how we can apply these dynamics to several strategic areas. I have identified five general areas where I desire to see God intervene on a daily basis, and where I believe, he desires to see his will accomplished. We will explore two of these areas in the remainder of this chapter and the other three in the next.

AREA ONE: PRAYING FOR OUR PERSONAL LIVES

Jesus Christ has given us permission to seek divine intervention in our personal lives. He delights in our desire to experience his intervention. Consequently, part of our time in prayer should be devoted to praying for our own personal spiritual needs. We can begin by affirming that we desire to experience the reality of God's kingdom in our lives and that we joyfully relinquish ourselves to God's purposes. Then we need to decide which specific dimensions of our spiritual lives we will pray about on a regular basis.

Early in my experience of building a more effective prayer life I had an encounter with God in this area. As I thought and prayed about where I needed intervention in my own life, a question entered my mind. The question was, "What do you want?" I had the sense the question was coming from God. The question was followed by the memory of James 4:2. That text says that often the reason we don't have something is because we have not asked God. The following verse in James reminds us that sometimes we ask for something and don't receive it because we ask with wrong motivation. I began to realize that there were many things I would like to see God do in my life that flow from proper motivation and are fully consistent with God's revealed will. I began to make a list of these desires that became a tool for praying about my spiritual needs.

There are things I pray for nearly daily. Here are a few:

To experience God's love.
To be an object of his favor.
To experience God's blessing.
To be a source of blessing to others.
To be filled with the Holy Spirit.
To stay in the flow of the Spirit.
To keep Christ on the "throne" of my life.
To be a "pencil" in God's hand.
To be in the center of his will.
To be obedient.

Stop and think about your own life. What do you want? Aren't there areas of your life where you would love to see God work? When you realize that these areas are consistent with God's revealed will, you can have confidence to pray for these things without feeling self-centered. God *wants* to intervene in our lives. It pleases him that we would desire to be the kind of men and women he wants us to be. Having prayed about our own spiritual needs, we can move on to a second area in which God's divine intervention is needed on a daily basis.

AREA TWO: PRAYING FOR YOUR FAMILY

I am a husband and a father. I have no greater privilege and responsibility than to pray for my wife and my children. Since I am also now a grandfather, I will add my grandchildren to that statement. It boggles the imagination to think about how the quality of our family life can be affected by exercising this privilege. Not to take advantage of this opportunity seems to violate the covenants and commitments I made when I decided to marry and have children. I wonder how different our world would look if more moms and dads were faithful in praying for their marriages and families. Families today are under tremendous pressure from the values of contemporary culture. The very word "family" means something radically different in the world than it did a decade ago. Powerful spiritual forces are at work to destroy God's foundational institutions like the family.

A number of years ago a friend of mine and his wife were flying back to Denver after a business trip. A young woman sat in the window seat next to his wife. When the flight attendant brought their meals (remember when meals were included in the cost of your airline ticket?) the young woman declined, stating with what my friend described as a prideful and even arrogant attitude, that she was fasting. After the attendant left, my friend's wife turned to the young woman and asked if she was fasting because she was a Christian. The woman laughed in her face. She informed my friends that not only was she not a Christian, she was a Satanist. She told them she and her coven were fasting and praying for the destruction of Christian marriages. She then added, "Especially the marriages of Christian ministers!" My friends were gob smacked to say the least.

When they told me this story I had several reactions. A cold chill ran down my spine and I became angry that such things could be true in modern America. Then I became convicted and embarrassed that someone who worshipped the devil took prayer more seriously than I often did.

The Bible clearly teaches that our struggles are not merely a matter of physical realities, but also of spiritual forces outside our conscious perception, (Ephesians 6:12). The real issues and battles are often decided in the heavenly arena. The vitality and welfare of our marriages and families are being affected by unseen realities that are powerfully influenced by effective prayer.

When I pray for my wife, Allison, and the children, I pray specifically for each of them by name. I begin by praying something like:

Father, I pray for Allison today. I ask that the realities of your kingdom - your power intervening and impacting - would be at work in her life. Bless her, Father. Give her rich spiritual prosperity. Protect her, Father. Work out your will in Allison's life today.

I then pray for the specific needs Allison is currently facing. In 1989, when I began to use this pattern, Allison was having a major struggle with depression. I began praying that she would be happy, that she would experience a fresh sense of her worth to God, and that her sense of esteem would come from her relationship with Christ. I prayed that she would be the queen of our house and that God would be glorified in our marriage. Once, as I was reading Isaiah 61:3, I sensed that I should pray this verse of scripture on behalf of Allison. I began to pray that God would bless her with "the crown of beauty, the oil of gladness, and a garment of praise."

In retrospect, it is amazing to see how God answered these requests. I have to say that he certainly didn't answer them in the way I would have planned. As I started praying, Allison got worse! But while her condition grew more serious, answers started to come. Along with her depression, she was having intense internal pain. Her doctor discovered that there was an existing physical reason for her problems that was treatable. Subsequently, Allison had the first of three major surgeries. Much of her depression was biochemically produced by her medical problems. Even though she has had her normal ups and downs through the years, the quality of her life, and our marriage, was radically changed for the better. God answered prayer.

During these same years, our marriage was significantly enriched. Again, let me say how God answered prayer is not exactly how I would have planned. But the bottom line is that our marriage became more mature and loving.

As I work on the update of this book, we face a new challenge. Over the last few years, Allison has developed memory problems. She has been diagnosed with Alzheimer's disease. It has been a devastating time for us. It is a disease that at the time of writing has no cure. It is also a disease that I have never heard of God healing. But that is what I'm praying. I'm praying for a miracle of healing for her and the discovery of a cure for the disease. If you are reading this I would invite you to pray for her.

How we pray for each other is limited only by our creativity. The power of prayer can be a major factor in helping us make it through those tough times in marriage that we all go through. As we pray for our spouse, God will often show us our own attitudes and actions that need to be changed. If you want the kind of marriage God intended you to have, prayer will be a major factor in seeing that desire realized.

I am the father of two children. Both are now adults. I have prayed for them for many years and continue to do so. From the time they were children I have desired that they would experience God's kingdom in their lives and know and live out God's will for their lives. Over the years I have seen God answer multitudes of prayer for them.

When our son, Baker, was a year old he developed serious medical problems. One day I read Psalm 144. In verse 12 the psalmist wrote, "then our sons in their youth will be like well-nurtured plants, and our daughters will be like pillars carved to adorn a palace." I began to pray this verse for my children.

At a point when Baker's prognosis was not very encouraging, hundreds of people in our church began to pray for him faithfully. Allison and I had prayed for him, had the elders of the church pray for him, and even had people who supposedly had the gift of healing pray for him. God did not choose to use any of these prayers to bring immediate healing. I had not told our whole congregation how ill Baker was. With a difficult Thanksgiving at Children's Hospital ahead of us, I shared our struggle from the pulpit. That day an outpouring of prayer began.

Two weeks later, when Baker entered Children's Hospital for three days of intensive testing, there was a marked improvement. He began to thrive. His metabolism began to function properly. He started to become a well-nurtured plant. The doctors diagnosed him with a rare genetic disorder, but as he grew it became obvious that either he never had the disorder, or God healed him. I remember how the doctors cautioned us that he would probably never be strong enough to play sports. I thought about that caution the day he beat me down a ski slope at Winter Park. God used the prayers of the church to release his healing power in Baker's life.

When Baker and Stephanie were young children, the last act of my day was to sit in a rocking chair in their rooms with them on my lap. I would pray for them and then end my time of prayer with the Levitical blessing of Numbers, chapter six:

The Lord bless you and keep you:
The Lord make his face shine upon you
*   and be gracious to you;*
The Lord lift up the light of his countenance upon you
*   and give you his peace.*

These days, praying for my adult children, and now grandchildren, is a regular part of my routine.

Your children need you to pray for them. It doesn't matter if they are young and at home, or grown and living on their own. It is a crazy world they are living in and it is a tremendous privilege to pray for them.

When I reach this point in my prayer time, I have prayed about two of the most significant areas in my life. As you begin to put these ideas into practice you might discover how little time you have been giving to this incredibly important work of prayer.

Having prayed for divine intervention in my own life, and the needs of my family, I still have several areas where I want to pray, "Your kingdom come!" We'll look at those in the next chapter. I'll hold off giving you another assignment till you have finished that chapter.

CHAPTER 6

Experiencing Divine Intervention, Part Two

§

But the angel said to him: "Do not be afraid,
Zechariah; your prayer has been heard."

(*LUKE 1:13*)

HAVING PRAYED ABOUT YOUR OWN need for divine intervention and the spiritual needs of your family, you can now use this component of your prayer time to pray for God's divine intervention in the world. Jesus taught the disciples that they should pray that God's will would be done on earth just as it is always done in heaven, (Mt. 6:10).

We live in a time that is so chaotic and filled with so many difficulties that it is easy to forget that God is still at work in this crazy world. Not only is God at work, he has plans and purposes for our world that we cannot fully comprehend. In his divine sovereignty God decided to use people to accomplish his purposes. Prayer is one vehicle through which we participate in what God is doing and wants to do in our world. I am often asked, "If God is sovereign, why pray?" I like to answer by saying that the sovereign

God has sovereignly willed to be influenced by the prayers of his people. With this confidence, I begin my time of praying for the world by praying for the primary institution through which God has chosen to reveal the realities of his kingdom during this age: the church.

Area Three: Praying for the Church

Over the last forty-five years I have had the privilege of serving in six churches. I have been everything from a Youth Pastor to a Senior Pastor. It has been an adventure. Several of the churches I served in struggled. A couple thrived by human standards. I'm sure God judges churches differently than our culture does. I won't be surprised if when we "check in" the churches that God was most pleased with were ones that most of us thought were insignificant.

When I wrote the first edition of this book I was working at a church that had experienced explosive growth. For a number of years, it had been one of the ten fastest growing churches in America. Much of the dynamic growth could be traced to a faithful group of men and women who were committed to praying for the church. I have learned over the years that there is a degree of mystery to why some churches grow while others stagnate. I've given up trying to figure it out. But where there is life and health, regardless of size, you will find men and women who pray for their church.

I currently pastor a church that is the perfect size. You might wonder how many members we have. It is irrelevant. It is the perfect size because many of us have prayed that God would bring the people who are supposed to be part of the church and keep away those who are not. I learned that concept years ago from Francis Schaeffer. That was how they prayed at his retreat in Switzerland.

Our church is the perfect size because it is the exact size God wants it to be.

How should you pray for your church? Let me give you a couple of ideas. Pray for the leadership of your church. Church ministry is hard. Along with the normal demands of any organization, the church faces the reality of spiritual warfare. Often the target of that warfare is the pastor and staff members of the church. I'm told the average life expectancy of a pastor in a church is three and a half years. I'm also told that the most productive time of ministry in the life of the pastor of a church is between years seven and ten. Do you see the problem? I hope the statistic is correct since I just finished my eighth year at Highline Community Church!

Pray for your pastor. Pray for his marriage, his family, his health, his spiritual life, and any needs you are aware he has. Pray for protection from the forces of evil. Pray that God's kingdom would come on him and God's will would be done in the church. If you attend a church with multiple staff members, pray the same for them.

Pray for the lay leadership in your church. I find that when a man or woman steps into a position of leadership, they often face unusual difficulty. I don't doubt that Satan takes notice when we up our game by stepping into these roles. Pray that the lay leadership and the pastor have good relationships. One of the evil one's most effective strategies for making churches ineffective is to create tension and discord among the clergy and the lay leadership. I also have been told that most ministers leave the churches they are serving because of ten people. I don't know where that statistic comes from, but often a few of those ten are on the church board.

Pray that both pastors and lay leaders are refreshed by the Holy Spirit. Fatigue and burn-out are two of the main reasons men and women leave the ministry. It is easy to get so engaged in doing ministry that personal devotional time suffers. The primary "job" of your pastor is to abide in Christ, (John 15:5). Without maintaining a vital relationship with Jesus, it is impossible to have an effective ministry.

If you worship at a church that has a large staff, consider choosing a few staff members to pray for regularly. If others in the congregation do the same, you can cover the entire staff in prayer.

Pray that all leadership in the church would experience God's blessing, protection, fruitfulness, effectiveness and faithfulness. Remember to pray for their families also. This is often the area Satan targets in his efforts to destroy the church.

Pray for the spiritual health of the church body itself. Ask God to bring renewal to the church and revival to the ministry. Pray the church would grow in spiritual maturity, love, and effectiveness in its ministry. Ask the Holy Spirit to move in the church and provide for the needs it faces. Ask the Spirit to show you how else to pray for your church. He will honor that prayer and place in your heart, and on your mind, the things you need to pray about.

The big question to ask yourself is what do you want to see God do in and through your church. It is your church, you know. Pray that God's kingdom will come on your church and that his will be done through your church. We live in challenging times. The church of Jesus Christ faces unique challenges and opportunities. In order to maximize these opportunities, we need the Spirit of God to work in the Church (with a capital C) to create unity, purity, power, and love. It is my conviction that such a movement will be intimately related to the faithful prayers of the men and women who make up the body of Christ. Do you want to be part of something great for God? Then pray for your church.

Area Four: Praying for the Nation

Over the years I have had the good fortune to travel to many parts of the world. I have been to some of the greatest places in the world, and I have been to some of the neediest places. I've been to major cities such as Paris, London, Lisbon, Amsterdam, Barcelona, Athens, and Jerusalem. And I've also been to remote villages in India where I was told I was one of the first white people the villagers had ever seen.

Having had all these experiences, I know that the United States is the greatest nation in the world. But I also know that as a nation we live in critical times. The last few decades have been marked by significant declines in the morals and values that have made America great. This decline is primarily the result of the influence of a small minority of men and women who work harder to promote their value systems than we do.

I confess, I often have been negligent about praying for America. As I began to implement the strategy mapped out in this book, I began to set aside time to pray for our nation. In 2 Chronicles 7:14, a promise was made by God to the people of Israel. It was given at the time of the dedication of Solomon's Temple. I believe the principles contained in the promise hold for today. God said:

> *If my people, who are called by my name, will humble themselves and pray and seek my face and turn from their wicked ways, then I will hear from heaven and will forgive their sin and heal their land.*

Our nation is at a point where it faces one of two destinies: revival or destruction. Our nation needs the forgiveness and healing God spoke of in this passage. If we really care about America, we can follow this formula from the Old Testament. We can repent personally of any wicked ways. We can humble ourselves. And we can pray. We can pray for America.

When I pray for our country I pray for three areas of need. I pray for God's influence and intervention in the lives of the leadership of our land. As I write, we have just come through a major election. We have a new President. The potential to turn a corner and see significant positive change is at hand. We can influence that change through prayer.

I know the task of praying for our country's leaders can seem overwhelming. That is why I decided to set realistic goals and pinpoint specific men and women to pray for at each level of government. I specifically pray for the President, and the Senators and Congressional leaders from my state.

I also pray for specific issues our nation faces. In the same way we can feel overwhelmed at the thought of praying for our leaders, praying for all the issues of the day can be overwhelming. I again limit myself and pray for those things that most concern me and that I sense God laying on my heart.

AREA FIVE: PRAYING FOR THE WORLD

The final area to which I apply my privilege of asking for divine intervention is the world. I know that by now you are experiencing one of two responses to the application of this component of prayer. Some of you are probably feeling overwhelmed. We have covered an amazing amount of territory, and we are only half-way through the Lord's Prayer! The overwhelmed response needs to change into the second response. This is a recognition of how many critically important areas we could be praying about on a daily basis. It takes significant time to do justice to cover the things that are closest to our hearts, and God's heart. How can we do it? Perhaps by setting the alarm a bit earlier in the morning or turning off the television and using the time to pray.

Mother Teresa is one of my heroes of the faith. In an interview several years ago in *Time Magazine*, she referred to herself as "a pencil in the hand of God". She went on to explain, "He does the thinking. He does the writing." I believe that is what most of us desire to be. We want to be men and women used by God in significant ways to accomplish his plans and purposes. In the interview, she was asked about how she spent her days. One set of responses went like this:

Q: What did you do today?
A: I prayed.
Q: When did you start?
A: Half-past four. (am!)

That's how you become a "pencil in the hand of God". We probably aren't going to start at half-past four (unless it is pm!). But, we might remember Mother Teresa as we attempt to climb out of bed every morning for a time of prayer where we can seek God and ask for his divine intervention for a world in desperate need.

Given the immense needs of the world, I would again suggest that rather than letting the need overwhelm you, pick a number of issues and people you will pray for. You might have a heart for world hunger. Maybe you have a passion for world evangelization. Or maybe the issue that stirs your heart is the persecution of Christians around the world.

When you look at the book of Acts you can see how the effective evangelism of the early church was energized by prayer. We live in a time when Jesus' prophetic promise of his return could come at any time. Jesus told the disciples that the gospel message would be preached in all the world and then the end would come, (Matthew 24:14). Major mission agencies around the world are seeking to make sure that condition is met. Modern technology makes the task possible in our generation.

I have had the great privilege periodically to visit men and women on the international mission field. Although it seems like all ministries need financial support, I am always impressed that the thing these spiritual heroes desire above all is the faithful prayers of those who know of their work. The spiritual resistance they face, especially in places where the church faces great hostility, is immense.

We might not be able to pray for every missionary in the world, but we can pick a handful and pray faithfully and consistently for them. We can pray that God's kingdom would come on them by the power of the Holy Spirit, and that God's will would be accomplished in their work and in their lives.

Let me close this chapter with a story. When I added this component to my prayer time back in 1989 I decided to pray for several countries in which I have special interest. Because of my family's heritage, one of the countries I began to pray for was Germany. The day the Berlin wall came down I had a funny thought. I wondered how many other people had been praying for Germany, and the wall. I'm sure many had prayed fervently about this situation for years. I know that sometimes God responds to the single prayer of one of his children. At other times there seems to be some kind of "critical mass" of prayer that needs to be reached before God acts. I found myself humorously wondering whether

God needed just one more person praying to reach "critical mass" on the wall and if I might have been that person. Who knows? But we do know this, there are multitudes of "Berlin Walls" in the world today. And I know that we have the amazing privilege to appropriate divine intervention as we pray, "Your kingdom come... your will be done."

You now have an important assignment. It is time to take the insights you have gained in the last two chapters and translate them into your own prayer life. Much of the following assignment involves working in your notebook. If you take the time to develop this section of your notebook, you will have a valuable tool!

ASSIGNMENT FOUR:

1. Go to the page in your prayer notebook entitled "Experiencing Divine Intervention."
2. Ask the Holy Spirit to show you the areas of your own life in which you should seek divine intervention. Ask yourself the question, "What do I want God to do in my life?" What are the spiritual needs and kingdom issues I need to be praying about in my life?" Write your list under "A".
3. If you are married and have a family, do the above exercise for each member of your family. "Family" will be your "B" in your outline. Each member of your family becomes a sub-point under the "Family" heading.
4. In the same way, add sections on (C) your church, (D) the nation, and (E) the world.
5. Ask the Holy Spirit to help you pray five days this week.

6. Pray through the first three components of your prayer notebook, adding your requests for divine intervention.
7. Pray through the remaining components briefly as outlined in Chapter 2.
8. Read Acts, chapter 12, daily.

CHAPTER 7

Praying for Provision

§

My God will meet all your needs...

(PHILIPPIANS 4:19)

JANUARY 1, 1980 MARKED THE beginning of a new decade. There is something about a new decade that makes us feel like the course of history is about to unfold new and exciting possibilities. That was certainly true for my wife and I. January 1, 1980 was the day our first child, Stephanie, was born. I became a father that day and my life has never been the same.

I remember holding Stephanie in my arms and wondering what this precious baby girl needed from a dad. I also remember walking out of the hospital that day and for the first time in my life worrying about the strangest thing: life insurance! Up until that day I was mostly concerned about making ends meet on a day-to-day and month-to-month basis. Allison and I had learned to live on very little and, at times, mostly on faith. But something happened the day I became a father. I became conscious of my responsibility to provide for my child. You see, by nature, fathers are hard-wired to be providers.

THE PRINCIPLE OF PROVISION

What is true of earthly fathers is also true of our heavenly father. He is concerned about our needs. His care for our needs is reflected in the instruction Jesus gave the disciples when he taught them to pray, "Give us this day our daily bread."

Again, notice the sequence of the things Jesus taught the disciples. For many of us our prayer time has primarily been focused on bringing our own needs to God. But Jesus taught the disciples that the Father knows our needs already, (Matthew 6:32). He also taught the disciples that preoccupation with our needs reveals a lack of trust in God as provider, (Matthew 6:25-32). Sequence becomes critical. Our priority is to pursue God's kingdom and righteousness, (Matthew 6:33). Even in coming to the Father for our own needs, we are to focus on God and his agenda.

A logical transition takes place at this point in the Lord's Prayer. The first phrases of the prayer all point to God. "Hallowed be *your* name...*your* kingdom come...*your* will be done." Now the topics have to do with *us*. Give *us* this day...forgive *us*...lead *us*. Having sought first the kingdom in prayer, it is now appropriate to turn our attention to our own needs.

At an earlier point in the strategy we thanked God for his providing nature. When we focused on God, using the *YHWH* names as a tool, we acknowledged that God is *YHWH-rohi*, "the Lord is my shepherd". One of the dimensions of God's shepherding role in our lives is to lead us to green pastures and quiet waters. The shepherd God is a provider. He is the source of our provision. More specifically, we have given thanks that he is *YHWH-jireh*, "the Lord will provide".

Israel's history demonstrates that the lesson of provision is one of the most important lessons we learn in our spiritual pilgrimage. This truth was certainly demonstrated during Israel's exodus from Egypt. It didn't take long for the provisions brought out of Egypt to run out. Moses and the people expected a relatively quick trip across the Sinai Peninsula and into the land of Canaan. Unfortunately, what should have been about a two-week journey turned into forty years of wandering. During those forty years God provided supernaturally for the nation. Six days a week, when the dew dried off the ground, a thin flaky substance was left on the desert floor. God called it "bread from heaven", (Exodus 16:4). When the people saw it they asked, "What is it?" In Hebrew, the question could be transliterated as *"Man hu?"* Eventually, they called the substance *"man ha,"* roughly meaning, *"It is what it is".*

God's instruction was clear, "Each one is to gather as much as he needs (for a day)," (Exodus 16:16). No one was to gather a surplus. When they did, it rotted. This was to be a day-by-day experience of trusting in God's provision. I'm sure Jesus had this in mind when he taught the disciples to pray for *daily* bread. God faithfully provided manna for forty years.

After forty years, a new generation prepared to enter the Promised Land under the leadership of Joshua. In his final message to the nation, Moses reminded this new generation of the provision of God and what it was intended to teach:

> *Remember how the Lord your God led you all the way in the desert these forty years, to humble you and to test you...He humbled you, causing you to hunger and then feeding you with manna... to teach you that man does not live on bread alone but on every word that comes from the mouth of the Lord,*
>
> (Deuteronomy 8:2-3).

God had been teaching the nation the lesson of provision. His covenant is one of provision. Therefore, as his children, we are to depend on him as the source of our security. We are to ask him to meet our needs.

I know people who think it is inappropriate to ask God to provide for their needs. They think it is selfish. They have been taught that in prayer we should only submit to God's will and be content with our circumstances. There is a small degree of truth in this way of thinking. It also has the appearance of great humility and spirituality. The problem with this way of thinking is that it is not totally biblical. The Bible instructs us to ask for what we need and pray about every area of life that produces anxiety. God *delights* in our dependence on him as the source of our provision. The Bible evens says that at times the reason we don't have what we need is that we haven't asked for it, (James 4:2).

PRINCIPLES OF PROVISION

As we enter into this period of our prayer time, and seek God's provision for our lives, it is important to understand certain principles that apply to receiving our "daily bread." God's provision is one area of our spiritual lives that is conditional. If we meet God's conditions, we can have confidence that he will provide. If we fail to meet certain conditions, God might choose to teach us by withholding his provision.

The first principle of provision is nearly self-evident. To be assured of God's provision in our lives, we need to be in a proper relationship with God. The promise of provision is for those with whom God has a father-child relationship. We must be Christians, in the biblical sense of the word, and have entered into a relationship with Jesus Christ as our lord and savior, resulting in the Holy Spirit invading our lives.

Along with having a father-child relationship with God, it is important that we are in a state of fellowship with Christ in order to receive his provision for our daily lives. By this point in our prayer time we are probably experiencing authentic spiritual communion with Christ. This fellowship will be further enhanced through consistent reading and study of God's Word.

Prayer and Bible study go hand-in-hand to produce a balanced life of fellowship with Christ. Prayer and Bible study should result in a life of joyful, willing, and disciplined obedience. If we are not in daily fellowship with the Lord, he might choose to withhold his provision as a means of getting our attention so that we examine our relationship with him.

One of the primary areas of obedience upon which God seems to condition his provision is our obedience in the area of financial stewardship. Faithfulness and obedience in giving are intimately related throughout the Bible to our own experience of God's provision. If our use of the resources God has already provided does not reflect our understanding and commitment to his ownership and lordship, God is in no way obligated to continue providing for us. The message of the Bible is very clear on this point: "Give, and it will be given to you," (Luke 6:38).

One of my favorite illustrations of this truth is found in the Old Testament book of Haggai. Haggai was a prophet sent by God to minister to the people of Israel after they had returned from their seventy-year exile in Babylon. God allowed their defeat and captivity as discipline for their continual idolatry and immorality during the previous years. He also crushed their false confidence in their empty religiosity by letting the Babylonians destroy the holy city of Jerusalem, including Solomon's Temple.

After seventy years, God began to bring the Israelites back to Jerusalem to rebuild the city, its walls, and the Temple. At the time of Haggai's ministry, the people had been back in the land for sixteen years. The primary reason for this first wave of return was to rebuild the Temple. Yet, after sixteen years they had barely started the work. Instead, the resources God had supplied to build the Temple had been used to construct their own homes. In what is surely an early example of spiritualizing blatant disobedience, the people justified their behavior by saying, "The time has not yet come," (to build the Temple) (Haggai 1:2). They were living a life of misplaced priorities and they were experiencing the consequences. God sent Haggai to the people with the simple message, "Consider your ways!" (Haggai 1:5,7).

This generation of God's people, after learning the hard lessons of captivity was still not fulfilling the conditions necessary to receive God's provision. The results of their disobedience in the area of stewardship were profound:

You have planted much, but harvested little. You eat, but never have enough. You drink but never have your fill. You put on clothes, but are not warm. You earn wages, only to put them in a purse with holes in it,

(Haggai 1:6).

God withheld his provision because of their misplaced priorities. Sound familiar? The text could have been written to many people today. It seems that some things never change.

The book of Haggai is one of the few instances in the Old Testament where the people actually listened to a prophet and did what God instructed. By the twentieth day of the same month the people had started to work on the house of the Lord, (Haggai

1:14-15). Their obedience was richly rewarded. God spoke several messages to them. He said, "I am with you," (Haggai 1:13, 2:4). He also said, "I will bless you," (Haggai 2:19). And finally, he said, "I will provide for you," (Haggai 2:15-19).

Our failure to meet the conditions of God's provision in our lives will have the same effect. If we rob God (see Malachi 3:8), we rob ourselves. If, on the other hand, we demonstrate our dependence and trust in God through faithful stewardship, we will be blessed (see Malachi 3:10).

My wife and I have talked with couples over the years that say they cannot afford to tithe. Tithing means we give one-tenth of our income to the ministry and work of the church. We have learned over the past forty-plus years that we cannot afford *not* to tithe. We want to live within the sphere of God's kingdom provision. In order to assure that provision, we work diligently to meet the conditions of provision.

Money can be both a source of blessing and a curse in our lives. The choice is really up to us. If you are not willing to meet God's conditions, there is no reason to pray for his provision. But, if you are wise enough to believe that God is the source of every good and perfect gift, and if you will live in obedient fellowship with him, then you have been given the authority and privilege to pray for your daily bread.

DAILY BREAD

How should you pray for your daily bread? I use this time to pray about two general areas of personal concern. First, I pray about the real needs of my day. I am almost embarrassed about how good God has been to my family. I need not ask for daily bread but rather thank God that he has already provided it. I'm sure a day could come when, like George Mueller, my family and I might sit at an empty table and thank God that he is going to provide food for a meal. At present, I have a refrigerator well stocked with a week's worth of meals. I thank God that he has met our needs and I pray that he will continue to help us live in a way that keeps us in the flow of his kingdom provision for our lives.

During this time of prayer, I pray for any specific physical or financial needs we might be facing as a family. I also use this time to pray about the other needs of my day. If it is a day when I am preparing to teach, I pray about my need for the Lord to provide good content and help me prepare. I also pray my presentation will be Holy Spirit empowered. If it is a day when I'm feeling tired and worn out, I pray God will provide some "green pastures" and some "quiet waters". I ask him to restore my soul. I simply ask myself the question, "What is my 'daily bread' today?" Then I pray about the need of the hour. I have learned to be specific about these needs because I believe that is how the Bible teaches us to pray.

The second area I pray about during this time is the area of *desires* and *anxieties*. We all have many desires and sources of concern in our lives that really don't fall under the category of "need". Yet, in both the gospels and the epistles we are instructed not to worry about our lives, (Matthew 6:25-34; Philippians 4:6-7). The biblical antidote for anxiety is prayer.

When I first started using this pattern of prayer I made a list of all the sources of desire and anxiety in my life. If I wanted it, or worried about it, I prayed about it. Some of what I pray about does seem trivial in the big picture of life, but not unimportant to a Father who cares about the most minute details of our lives.

I pray cautiously. I am always reminded of the time in the wilderness when the nation of Israel became discontent with manna and asked for meat. The answer to this prayer created a disaster. The psalmist wrote that God gave them what they craved, but sent leanness into their souls, (Psalm 106:15). I would rather not have what I want if it is not God's perfect will. I pray for what I want, but ask God not to give it to me if it would bring "leanness into my soul".

Having prayed through both my needs and my concerns I almost always come to the end of this component of prayer with a sense of peace. I have been with my heavenly father who is *YHWH-jireh*, "the Lord who provides". I have sought first his kingdom and his righteousness in prayer. I have sought to meet the conditions of fellowship and obedience that govern the giving of his kingdom provision. I have come with faith and expectation, setting before him my needs, desires and concerns. I thank him that he is the source of my security and the source of my provision. With all these issues behind, I am ready to move on to the next component of prayer.

The Notebook

Before we move on, let me make a few more comments about your notebook. When I began writing down my strategy in a notebook I had no idea how helpful this tool would become. I tried a notebook approach before, but usually it simply consisted of a series of lists I was asking God to do something about. The notebook I am asking you to develop is much more than that.

One of the big problems many men and women have in praying consistently and effectively is a lack of focus and the problem of distraction. For many, simply sitting with their eyes closed and trying to remember everything they need to pray about leads to distraction and fatigue. A good notebook keeps you focused. I am constantly adding to each category biblical references and personal insights. At times, I actually sit with a pen or pencil in my hand and point to each line in the notebook as I pray. If you want to get the most out of using this strategy…do the assignments and build your notebook.

ASSIGNMENT FIVE:

1. Develop the "Praying for Provision" section in your notebook.
    a. Under "A", list the *needs* of your life you desire God to meet.
    b. Under "B", list the *desires* of your life that you would like to see God give you.
    c. Under "C", list the sources of *anxiety* in your life you would like to see God relieve.
2. Review the passages of scripture referred to throughout this chapter.
3. Pray through the first four components of prayer, integrating this chapter into your strategy.

CHAPTER 8

Experiencing Forgiveness

§

Blessed is he whose transgressions are forgiven.

(PSALM 32:1)

I LOVE BEING A CHRISTIAN. It is the ultimate no-lose proposition. All my life I have been involved in organizations and institutions based on performance. I played on athletic teams where my performance dictated my opportunity to participate. At the level where my performance peaked, I lost the opportunity to move to the next level of competition. My value as an athlete was based on my performance.

I also have twenty-five years of formal education under my belt. I can safely say I am educated beyond my level of intelligence! Academic achievement is based on performance. As long as I performed well I was able to advance academically and be rewarded with high grades and advanced degrees. Even in ministry my success or failure is based on my performance. If I perform well, and people are helped, I am praised and affirmed. When my performance slips, or I fail to communicate effectively, I receive criticism. Enough criticism and my job is at risk.

In virtually every area of our lives we are evaluated and rewarded on the basis of performance. This puts us all under incredible amounts of pressure. We all know that in every arena in which we perform we are eventually bound to fail. That is why I'm glad I am a Christian.

Becoming a Christian was the one experience of my life that was not based on my performance. I became a Christian on the basis of my failure and Jesus Christ's performance. The church is the one organization in the world that has as its criterion for membership our corporate failure. We come together because of our powerlessness and lack of performance. The ultimate motto of the church is "We are all bozos on this bus!"

Becoming a Christian is an act of grace – God's grace. The Bible says, "By grace you have been saved…" (Ephesians 2:8). Grace is God's unmerited, undeserved, unearned favor. It is a gift. In grace, the Father sent his only son to die an atoning death for the forgiveness of sin and to make possible the gift of salvation. I am a moral, ethical, and spiritual failure. In either attitude or action, I have broken all of God's absolute imperatives expressed in the Ten Commandments. If I had to perform to earn a relationship with God I would be in big trouble. The good news (the meaning of the Greek word we translate "gospel") proclaims the fact that I am not accepted on the basis of my performance. I am accepted, once for all time, on the basis of God's grace and Christ's work on the cross. That is why I love being a Christian.

There is obviously much more to being a Christian than the initial experience of receiving God's grace. When I received the gift of grace, a permanent transaction took place that will never change for all eternity. The biblical term used to describe this transaction is *justify*, meaning "to declare righteous." In the instant this transaction occurred, I experienced the invasion of my inner life by the Holy Spirit. The Holy Spirit brought new life where there was spiritual death. He regenerated my human spirit by his presence.

With this new life, a process of transformation began. God began to work within me to change my character so that I might become more like Christ. The transformation process is intimately related to my daily relationship with God. My daily relationship with God is not like the once-and-for-all transaction of justification. My daily experience is related to my performance. When I fail, fellowship with God is impaired. Because of my tendency to fail, I need a means for my ongoing failures to be brought under the once-and-for-all atonement of Christ. Just as I need daily bread, I need daily grace.

To facilitate the experience of daily grace, Jesus taught the disciples that one of the primary components of their prayer life was to be a time of confession and forgiveness. He instructed them to pray, "Forgive us our sins," (Luke 11:4). Forgiveness is the next component in our strategy.

THE REALITY OF SIN

Have you ever been in a worship service where several groups of Christians were meeting together and using the Lord's Prayer as a liturgical prayer? Everyone is boldly praying aloud until they come to this line in the prayer. Suddenly, you can feel the anxiety begin to build. What are we going to pray? Will it be "forgive us our debts", "forgive us our trespasses", "forgive us our sins", or some new request for forgiveness that we have not yet encountered? Usually you end up with some mumbled combination of all of the above. Why all the confusion? The answer is that in the Bible itself two different words are used in the two places where we find the Lord's Prayer.

Jesus actually taught this prayer on two separate occasions. The version contained in Matthew's gospel is part of the Sermon on the Mount. Here he was speaking to a large group of his followers. In Luke's account, he was speaking to his twelve disciples who had asked him to teach them to pray. Since Jesus was probably speaking in Aramaic, it is hard to know if he used different words, or whether Matthew and Luke, writing in Greek, used different words to translate and record what he said.

In Luke's account the word translated "sin" is the Greek word *hamartia*. This is the most generic word used in the New Testament to communicate the concept of moral, ethical, or spiritual failure. The literal meaning of the word is "to miss the mark". The "mark", or biblical standard for the conduct of life is the very nature of God himself. When our lives fail to measure up to the holiness and perfection of God's character we "miss the mark" - in other words, we sin. Sometimes our missing the mark is an unintentional violation of some boundary God has established. Such violations, without premeditated willfulness, are called "trespasses". Other times our violations of the boundaries involve a degree of knowledge and willfulness. In such cases, the harsher word "transgression" is a more appropriate translation. Often, we simply fail by not doing what ought to be done. We "fall short" of the standard.

In all of these instances, we have a problem. We create what Francis Schaeffer used to call "true moral guilt." By that term, Schaeffer was making a distinction between the emotional experience of guilt feelings - which may or may not be related to some moral, ethical, or spiritual failure - and true guilt, which is a product of an actual violation of God's standards. True moral guilt is a product of the truth that all of us have "missed the mark" and habitually are "falling short" of God's standards, (Romans 3:23).

Recognizing and acknowledging this fact is critically important, as painful as it might be, for a healthy, daily relationship with God. This component of our prayer time forces us to get honest with God and with ourselves.

GUILT AND FORGIVENESS

I was motivated to go on my twenty-one-day solitude experience for a number of reasons. I was at a point in my life where I felt like I needed a spiritual breakthrough. I was feeling spiritually and emotionally burned out. This condition was having a negative impact on many of my relationships, especially my marriage. My wife helped me see that whenever we entered into conflict my responses to her were becoming verbally abusive. I rationalized my behavior by assuring her that I was only attempting to be honest about my feelings.

It took nearly a week in isolation for God to penetrate what I have come to think of as "filters". These are the internal hindrances that keep God from breaking through to us at a greater experiential level. I am convinced, having experienced what I did, that these hindrances to experiencing the more direct presence of God are rarely penetrated apart from prolonged times of retreat and solitude. This has been the historic experience of the spiritual fathers of the church throughout the centuries.

At the end of my first week on Fox Island I had the first of several experiences that took me to a new level of spiritual encounter. The first experience came in the context of dealing with sin in my life. God gave me a true understanding about what I was doing in my relationship with Allison. With great clarity, I understood how I was being emotionally and verbally abusive to her. I had a very clear sense of how painful and destructive my behavior was. My understanding was infused with the deepest experience of conviction I have ever felt in my life. I fell to the floor and wept with a sorrow that transcended any I had ever known. It was gut wrenching.

What followed was amazing. I felt the touch of God in a way that is difficult to describe. As I shared at the beginning of this book, it was as if the core of my being was penetrated by his being. What I experienced was felt grace. I felt God's love breaking through. I was overwhelmed. Where I expected condemnation, I received love. I deserved condemnation, but I received grace. The power of this reality was even stronger than the pain of conviction.

Following this experience, I reflected on how deceived I had been about my sin. Henry David Thoreau is known for the famous quote, "Most men lead lives of quiet desperation." Let me suggest a deeper problem of the human condition: most men and women lead lives of destructive self-deception. Very few people take sin seriously. We treat it as a small problem to be dealt with in trivial ways. But this is not the case. It cost Jesus his life to provide a solution to the sin problem.

Futile Solutions

Since every person on the planet has the problem of true moral guilt, everyone has the need for forgiveness. Every religious and philosophical system in the world attempts to define what people need to do to deal with the problems and difficulties of existential angst that plague unredeemed humanity.

There are those who worship at the shrine of education. They tell us that what people really need is more information. The modern gurus of Eastern philosophy, in its many forms and manifestations, tell us we need to discover our innate deity and escape the world of material illusion by experiencing oneness with god ("god" being a convenient word used to mean both everything and nothing).

The modern Pharisees assure us that we only need to do more "good" things than "bad". The modern materialists declare that more of the right "stuff" will solve our problems. Every system has a solution. There is only one problem: all these philosophical and religious systems still leave us with true moral guilt. True moral guilt alienates us from God, from one another, and ultimately alienates us even from ourselves. Everyone deals with this issue in one way or another.

Many people handle guilt by repressing or internalizing it. But guilt is like a cancer that eats away at the human psyche and ultimately destroys us. Others attempt re-education as the solution. They advocate that guilt is simply the product of faulty programming in the human unconscious. Some seek to atone for their guilt by becoming religious, or working at humanitarian causes. Tragically, some men and women deal with guilt by punishing themselves with myriad forms of self-abuse, from the blatant chemical abuse of drugs and alcohol to the more complicated forms of self-hatred like depression and low self-esteem. The problem with all these solutions is the same...*they don't work!* There is only one effective solution for true moral guilt. That solution is now accessible through prayer.

FORGIVENESS

Jesus taught the disciples to pray, "Forgive us our debts, as we also have forgiven our debtors," (Matthew 6:12). The word translated "debt" here is the Greek word *opheilema*. In most cases, it refers to one person owing money to another. In Matthew 6 it is used metaphorically of a debt we owe in our relationship with God. The most vivid biblical illustration of this concept is found in Colossians 2:13-14.

In this text, Paul writes that through the cross of Christ the written charge against us has been cancelled. The word translated "written charge" is the Greek word *cheirographon*. It was primarily a business term used in the first century for a note or certificate of debt. It is synonymous with the Greek word *epigraphon* that was used when referring to the list of charges drawn up against a convicted criminal in the Roman court system.

In the Roman business world, when the debt had been paid, a word was written across the note of debt. The word was the Greek word *tetelesthai* meaning "paid in full." The certificate with "paid in full" was a receipt guaranteeing no further payments were necessary.

In the Roman judicial system, when punishment for a crime had been fulfilled, the same word was written across the list of charges, releasing the convicted criminal from any further punishment. In capital offenses, the Romans would nail the written charge to the top of the cross when the sentence called for crucifixion. That way all who passed by the hideous scene would know what led to this person's execution. You might imagine that this approach was a powerful deterrent to crime! We are told that when Jesus Christ was crucified as a common criminal, Pilate had a written charge (*epigraphon*) drawn up and affixed to his cross. Pilate had found no guilt in Jesus, so the written charge read:

This is Jesus, the King of the Jews,

(Matthew 27:37).

These were the words people would read as they passed by the cross of Christ that day so long ago. But from God's perspective something much more significant was taking place. What Paul tells us in Colossians 2:13-14 is that from God's perspective it was our written charge, our *cheirographon* that was nailed to the cross of Christ. You might conceptualize this as a document containing every failure on our part to meet God's standards morally, ethically, or spiritually in attitude, action, or intent. This certificate is a history of all the sin, trespass, and transgression of our lives - past, present, and future. For most of us, this would be a long and ugly document.

When Jesus Christ was crucified, this document was nailed to the cross with him. Our sin is the true reason Jesus suffered such a brutal execution. He was paying the price to cancel our certificate of debt. Just before Jesus died we are told that he cried out from the cross. Most translations read that his cry was, "It is finished," (John 19:30). But if you look at the Greek text, you will find that this cry was actually one word. Jesus cried out, *"Tetelesthai!"* "Paid in full" was the triumphant declaration Jesus made with his dying breath. In that instant, God took our certificate of debt and cancelled it. You can think of it as God writing across the record of our sin, *"Tetelesthai."*

EXPERIENCING FORGIVENESS

When you embrace Jesus Christ as Savior and Lord, you appropriate his finished work on your behalf. Your sins are forgiven. Guilt is removed and your conscience is cleansed. If you have authentically repented and received Christ's forgiveness, any further feelings of guilt are not a product of true moral guilt. When we do sin, we are called to confront our sin honestly. The Holy Spirit working within us will convict us when we again "miss the mark." Our appropriate response when this happens is to respond to this conviction by agreeing with the Spirit and acknowledging our sin.

The Greek word for confession, *homologeo*, literally means "to say the same thing." When we sincerely confess, and repent, we can instantly experience the forgiveness and spiritual cleansing Jesus provided for us by his atoning death. God promises:

> *If we confess our sins, he is faithful and just and will forgive us our sins and purify us from all unrighteousness,*
>
> *(I John 1:9).*

During this period of your prayer time I would suggest working through four stages in order to both receive and dispense forgiveness.

STAGE ONE: GETTING HONEST

Confession is a time when we can be totally honest with God and ourselves. On a daily basis, we need to allow the Holy Spirit to show us areas of our life that need to be brought to Christ in confession. In the Psalms, David prayed:

> *Search me, O God, and know my heart;*
> *Test me and know my anxious thoughts.*
>
> *See if there is any offensive way in me,*
> *and lead me in the way everlasting,*
>
> (Psalm 139:23-24).

David recognized his need of God's help in this area of spiritual restoration. Knowing the tendency of the human ego to be blind to its own shortcomings and sins, David also prayed:

Who can discern his errors?
Forgive my hidden faults.
Keep your servant also from willful sins,

(Psalm 19:12-13).

As I get honest with God, I ask the Holy Spirit to show me specific sins I need to confess. I thank God for his grace and the atoning work of Christ which covers my sins. In my prayer notebook, I have also made a list of the flaws in my character that seem to be ongoing sources of struggle in my life. I pray about these on a regular basis.

STAGE TWO: CONFESSION

Having invited God to search me and make known anything needing confession, I confess. I agree with the Holy Spirit about my sin. Confession is cathartic. It is like breathing out carbon dioxide in order to fill our lungs with fresh air.

When my wife was pregnant with our daughter, and later our son, we went through childbirth classes together. I imagine many of you have done the same. Allison learned to breath in a way that helped controlled the pain of the labor process. During one stage of breathing she was to follow a series of short, quick breaths with one long, lung-emptying expulsion of air. This breath was called a "cleansing breath." That is what confession is like. It is God's provision for spiritual cleansing.

Sometimes it is helpful to confess not only to God, but also to another human being. Those within the Catholic tradition have always used the ministry of the priest as the one to whom sin is confessed and through whom forgiveness is mediated. Those of us within the Protestant world have grown up in a spiritual climate where confession is primarily addressed to God without an intermediary. But we also recognize a theological principle called the priesthood of all believers (see 1 Peter 2:9). In response to James 5:16, we should acknowledge the value of sharing our struggles and failures with brothers or sisters (depending on your gender) who can support and encourage us on our spiritual journey. A small group that is committed to confidentiality is a great place for this to take place.

STAGE THREE: CHANGE

Part of the good news about the good news is that it includes the power to see our lives changed. Confession is not an end in itself. Confession clears the decks so that God can work to change my life. I fully expect that over time God is going to work in my life to bring about transformation in the areas of my character that cause me consistent struggle. In order for that change to occur, I have to be willing. Perhaps you have heard the joke: "How many psychiatrists does it take to change a light bulb?" The answer: "Only one, but the light bulb really has to want to change!" The spiritual life is like that.

We need to desire to be the men and women God desires us to be. Are we willing to let God change us? Our time of confession is a time when we call upon the power of God to change the defects of our character and the patterns of our lives that do not conform to his will. By nature, we drift toward sin. Only the power of God, released through my willingness, can overcome that tendency. The battle is won or lost one day at a time. That is why daily confession is so important.

STAGE FOUR: FORGIVENESS AND RESTITUTION

In the Lord's Prayer, Jesus attaches another condition to our experience of forgiveness. Not only are we to confess our sins, we are to be willing to forgive those who have sinned against us. Sometimes our sin is very personal and only involves ourselves and God. At other times, our sin inflicts pain and damage on other people. Sometimes, the sins of other people inflict pain and damage on us.

When we are the object of another's sin, it is human nature to become bitter and harbor resentment. We often nurse our anger until it brews and boils. Eventually, we find ourselves wishing ill of the one who offended us. Our inner life becomes filled with negative emotion. Often the damage caused to our sense of peace and well-being by our bitterness is more destructive than the original offense.

Understanding the impact of negative emotions, Jesus taught the disciples to practice a discipline of forgiveness. Having received grace, we are to dispense grace. Part of our time of prayer is to be focused on remembering who has offended us and then making a conscious decision to forgive them. At the feeling level, we might still struggle with the one who has offended us, but as we *consistently* will to forgive, God is set free to diffuse and disperse the negative emotion.

When our sin has caused emotional, spiritual, or physical damage to another, we need to make restitution. Restitution means that we attempt to make things right. Sometimes that requires going to the one we have offended and asking for forgiveness. Sometimes that means we actively seek to restore anything that was damaged or lost in our act of sin.

The forgiveness component of our prayer time can be incredibly liberating. It is reconstruction time for a life ill-lived. It brings into our experience not only the love and grace of God, but also his incredible, transforming power. It provides us with the guidance, motivation, and enabling power to reconcile our relationships with

God and with others. It enables us to live with the experience of inner cleansing and the peace of God that accompanies such a spiritual state. Take this time seriously and I promise, you will reap the benefits.

Now it is time for you to go to work. Go to the page in your notebook labeled "Experiencing Forgiveness" and work through the following exercises:

Assignment Six:

1. Alternate reading Psalm 51 and Psalm 32 every day this week.
2. Under "A" in your outline, make a list of the ongoing problems of your character which give you the greatest problems (i.e. envy, lust, coveting, greed, etc.)
3. Ask the Holy Spirit to show you specific sins that need confession. Be open and honest.
4. Confess (agree with) what he shows you. Thank Jesus for his forgiveness.
5. Under "B" in your outline, make a list of those people who have "sinned against" you. Remember to include mothers, fathers, husbands, wives, sisters, and brothers. Make a decision to begin to forgive these offenses.
6. Ask the Holy Spirit to reveal to you any people to whom you need to make restitution and what that restitution needs to be.
7. Make restitution.
8. Ask the Holy Spirit to help you pray consistently at least five days this week.
9. Pray through your notebook outline, adding this section on forgiveness.

CHAPTER 9

Developing Spiritual
Protection

§

The Lord is my rock, my fortress and my deliverer,

(PSALM 18:2)

ONE OF MY FAVORITE TIMES of the day is early morning. I love
waking up before anyone else in the family. My favorite mornings are the ones when I realize upon waking that I don't have to
rush off to an early morning meeting or appointment. On those
mornings, I know I can spend time sitting in my favorite chair in
the living room and enjoy the beauty of a Colorado morning. As
I stumble out of bed and head toward the living room I usually
have one thing on my mind - coffee! My wife, Allison, and I have
become moderate coffee snobs. We now grind our own beans and
French press our morning coffee. There is nothing like a great cup
of coffee on an early morning.

Part of what I enjoy about my first cup of coffee is the cup itself. Over the years Allison and I have collected an assortment of
colorful and humorous coffee mugs. Some mornings, just looking

at my coffee mug and getting a small chuckle out of it seems to get my day off to a positive start. For instance, one of our mugs has two cartoon deer engaged in conversation. One of the deer has what appears to be a large, red and white, bullseye on his chest. The other deer, looking at the bullseye, comments, "Bummer of a birthmark, Hal!"

This morning I was drinking from a mug that has a series of wild animals dressed in suits, carrying briefcases, heading into a metropolitan scene, complete with skyscrapers. The caption on this mug is written inside the rim of the cup so that it faces you when you take your first drink. In large capital letters this mug reminds its user, "It is a jungle out there." This mug not only makes me smile, it reminds me of one of the reasons why I need to combine my morning coffee with a hearty time of prayer. It *is* a jungle out there. Actually, it is even more dangerous than a jungle. A jungle is full of known, and at times dangerous, natural enemies. The world in which we live is filled with unknown and dangerous supernatural enemies. Maybe we should all have a mug that reminds us that it is a *battlefield* out there! Our mug could be inscribed with Paul's message to the Ephesians:

> For our struggle is not against flesh and blood, but against the rulers, against the authorities, against the powers of this dark world and against the spiritual forces of evil in the heavenly realms,
> (Ephesians 6:12).

We live in a supernatural universe, engaged in spiritual battle. In light of this reality, there are certain critically important concepts we need to master in order to win this battle.

I remember living through the turmoil of the Vietnam War. I was in high school and college during those years and never actually fought in the war. But as a student, I was right in the middle of the debate about the war here at home. During those years, there were many popular mottoes and slogans expressing both sides of the opinions surrounding the conflict. Anti-war protesters wore t-shirts exhorting America to "Make love, not war." Pro-war advocates displayed bumper stickers advising Americans to "Love it, or leave it." One of the more popular slogans of the era forced a bit of philosophical reflection. It asked the question on posters, t-shirts, and bumper stickers across America: "What if they gave a war and no one came?" Perhaps that was an option with Vietnam, but it certainly is not an option with the war in which we are engaged.

Like it or not, we are part of a war of epic and eternal significance that affects every area of our lives. This war is often remarkably subtle. For many men and women, the unfortunate motto of this war could be: "What if you were in a war and didn't even know it?" Many men and women are casualties of a war they don't know is being waged. This ought not be the case. We are to be conscious of the reality of spiritual warfare. We are to be prepared and equipped to wage this war. To this end Jesus taught the disciples that one of the seven major components of prayer involved developing spiritual protection. He taught us to pray, "Lead us not into temptation, but deliver us from evil," (Matthew 6:13).

THE ENEMY: PART ONE

In the instruction Jesus gave about our need for spiritual protection, he identified the two greatest enemies we face in this area of spiritual warfare.

He first instructed the disciples to pray, "Lead us not into temptation." It is hard for many of us to admit that a part of our very nature is our enemy. Remember the old saying, "We have found the enemy, and it is us." It is this part of human nature that is so vulnerable to temptation. We need help to steer clear of the situations and circumstances that have the potential to derail our faith. In regard to temptation, the great Reformation theologian, Martin Luther, used to say that we can't keep the birds from flying over our heads, but we can keep them from building nests in our hair. Yet, Jesus seems to imply that in prayer we might be able to either change the "bird's" flight pattern, or at least our exposure to it.

In Romans, chapter seven, the Apostle Paul paints a vivid picture of our internal struggle. He declares, "I know that nothing good dwells in me, that is, in my flesh," (Romans 7:18). When Paul speaks of "flesh", he is not referring to the physical flesh of the human body. He is speaking about an internal propensity toward self-centeredness and sin which the Bible calls our old nature. This part of our inner being exists in a condition which C.S. Lewis, in his space trilogy, referred to as "bent." Almost every internal struggle we face in our spiritual lives is a product of this fallen dimension of our being.

In Galatians, chapter five, Paul describes the activities of this nature:

> *The acts of the "flesh" are obvious: sexual immorality, impurity and debauchery; idolatry and witchcraft; hatred, discord, jealousy, fits of rage, selfish ambition, dissensions, factions and envy; drunkenness, orgies, and the like,*
>
> (Galatians 5:19-21).

Before Jesus Christ invades our lives, we possess only one nature. We live under the dominant influence of the flesh. This nature is predisposed to sin. Sinning is easy; it comes *naturally*. When we invite Christ into our lives, the Holy Spirit creates a new nature within us by his presence and activity. When this occurs, we have the potential to produce the fruit of the Spirit instead of the deeds of the flesh. Notice the difference:

> *But the fruit of the Spirit is love, joy, peace, patience, kindness, goodness, faithfulness, gentleness and self- control,*
> (Galatians 5:22-23).

Every minute of every day we have the potential of allowing one of these two realities to dominate our lives. It is the old sin nature, the flesh, that is particularly susceptible to temptation. James writes:

> *When tempted, no one should say, "God is tempting me." For God cannot be tempted by evil, nor does he tempt anyone; but each one is tempted when, by his own evil desire, his is dragged away and enticed,*
> (James 1:13-14).

How do we overcome temptation? God has provided resources that will help. When Jesus was tempted in the wilderness, his consistent response to the Tempter was, "It is written!" He quoted scripture and responded in obedience to the truth contained in it to overcome Satan's temptations. In the same way, memorizing the Bible helps us fight temptation. The psalmist wrote: "I have hidden your word in my heart that I might not sin against you," (Psalm 119:11).

Finding God's provision out of temptation can also help us overcome sin. The Bible promises:

No temptation has seized you except what is common to man. And God is faithful; he will not let you be tempted beyond what you can bear. But when you are tempted, he will also provide a way out so that you can stand up under it,
(I Corinthians 10:13).

Sometimes, our way out is to exercise spiritual willpower to resist the temptation, (I Peter 5:9). At other times, the way out will be to turn from the temptation and flee. Your flight at times will be figurative, (2 Timothy 2:22). At other times, like Joseph, your flight might be quite literal, (Genesis 39:12).

Of all the resources God has provided for overcoming temptation, the most effective is avoidance. In the book of Proverbs, the smartest man in the world repeatedly exhorts his son to avoid the way of temptation, (see Proverbs 5,6, and 7).

That is why we are to pray "lead us not into temptation." One way to avoid the path of temptation is to seek, like David in the twenty-third psalm, to be guided to "paths of righteousness," (Psalm 23:3).

During this component of our prayer time we can begin by praying that God will guide our lives in such a way that we experience a minimum of temptation. We can also pray that as God leads us in paths of righteousness, he would help us lead obedient lives.

The spiritual armor in Ephesians, chapter six, has both defensive and offensive dimensions. Notice how those pieces which metaphorically speak of defense against attack all have to do with our character and lifestyle:

> *Therefore, put on the full armor of God, so that when the day of evil comes you may be able to stand your ground...Stand firm then, with the belt of **truth** buckled around your waist, with the breastplate of **righteousness** in place...take up the shield of **faith**, with which you can extinguish all the flaming arrows of the evil one. Take the helmet of **salvation**...,*
>
> (Ephesians 6:13-17).

Our prayer "closet" becomes a spiritual dressing room in which we "dress for success" in order to be prepared to resist sin and temptation.

THE ENEMY: PART TWO

The second part of this component of prayer is to be focused on Jesus' instruction to pray for deliverance from evil, (Matthew 6:13). The Greek text of this verse includes the definite article before the word evil. Literally, the text could be translated "deliver us from *the* evil." Because of the use of the article, many biblical scholars believe Jesus is not simply speaking of evil as a principle, but rather to evil personified. They would translate the verse, "deliver us from the evil one."

We not only have an internal enemy - our old fallen nature - in our battle to live the Christian life, we have a very real and personal external enemy. If there were a "Four Spiritual Laws" of spiritual warfare, the first law would be, "Satan hates you and has a diabolical plan for your life."

The authority Jesus has given us in prayer is a powerful weapon in overcoming the schemes and attacks of the evil one. I consider prayer about God's protection from Satan's attacks one of my greatest privileges and responsibilities.

Over the years, I have grown in my understanding of, and sensitivity to, spiritual warfare. I've also grown in my understanding and experience of the resources I have available to deal with Satan's schemes. I have come to understand something of the authority God has given the Christian, not only to stand and exercise authority in the face of evil, but the invitation he has given us to pray for spiritual protection to keep Satan from being able to gain access to our lives.

SPIRITUAL PROTECTION

Many years ago, I attended a series of seminars call "The Institute in Basic Youth Conflicts". I remember an illustration used in one session to depict the spiritual authority of the father in the family. The speaker used a picture of an umbrella to represent the protective authority of the father. When members of the family moved out from under the father's authority in rebellion or disobedience, they also moved out from underneath this umbrella of protection, becoming more susceptible to spiritual attack. When the father was out of fellowship with God, either through sin or negligence, his umbrella developed holes, making it possible for the evil one to gain access to those under the father's authority.

How do you put up a spiritual umbrella of protection? I believe we pray it into place. When we are instructed to pray "deliver us," the word used in the Greek text is *rhuomai*. The word not only means "deliver from," but also "preserve from" or "protect from."

There are many images in the Bible of how God provides spiritual protection for those who belong to him. By his presence and his power, he becomes a refuge or fortress to those who seek his protection, (see Psalms 27:1-6; 46:1; 91:1-2). As a mother bird protects her children by covering them with her wings, so God provides protective covering to those whom he loves, (Psalm 91:4).

One of the more vivid images of God's provision of supernatural protection is found in what some scholars believe to be the oldest book of the Bible. We are told that Job was an upright man who walked with God. In the unseen realm of heavenly realities, a dialogue occurred between God and Satan concerning Job, (Job 1:6-8). Satan, desiring to afflict Job, makes note of the fact that God had erected a "hedge" around Job, his household, and everything Job had, (Job 1:9). The story of Job tells how God removed that hedge and allowed Satan to attack Job. God allowed Job to suffer temporarily in order that he might experience a measure of spiritual growth and enlightenment that would last for all eternity.

The image of a hedge surrounding Job's life is a useful one in our prayer time. The historical setting of both the Old Testament and the New Testament is an agricultural one. Many biblical images were agricultural in nature because of their relevance to the initial recipient of God's message. When a farmer planted a vineyard in Israel, he would build a literal hedge around the vineyard to keep destructive predators out of the vineyard.

God often referred to Israel as his vineyard. He built a spiritual hedge around Israel to protect the nation. When Israel slipped into idolatry and immorality by worshipping the gods of other nations, God would remove his hedge and allow the nation to be attacked and defeated. In Isaiah's "Song of the Vineyard" (see Isaiah 5:1-7), God warned Israel that he was about to send judgment against the nation. He warned them by saying:

Now I will tell you
  What I am going to do to my vineyard:
  I will take away it's hedge,
  And it will be destroyed,

(Isaiah 5:5).

In prayer, we can erect a spiritual hedge around our lives and our families. Perhaps the image of a hedge is not as relevant in our technological age as it was in Isaiah's or Job's. I conceptualize this protective presence as a spiritual force field surrounding my life, my family, and my home. This force field is generated by the presence and power of God himself. In prayer, I appropriate his spiritual protection against evil and the evil one.

One of the more important insights I have gained about prayer in the last few years involves the immediacy with which God responds to prayer. The instant I pray for protection, it is in place. I know this by faith. When I neglect to pray for God's protective presence, I leave myself and my family open to spiritual attack. I believe God often protects, even when I am negligent to ask for it, but I know that when I do ask, he delivers!

I have a sense (without any scriptural validation) that protection is similar to provision. It seems to last about twenty-four hours. Day-by-day, I need to pray the hedge into place. When I have been negligent in this area, unexplained problems seem to develop. As I become aware of my negligence, I pray for God to drive out all the predators that have invaded my spiritual vineyard and shore up whatever breaches I have allowed to develop in my spiritual fortress.

The Host of Heaven

During this time of prayer, I have also started praying about the ministry of angels in their protective role. There has been a great deal of attention concerning the existence and role of angels in the last few years. Unfortunately, much of what has been written has come from people who have very little understanding or interest in what the Bible teaches about this subject.

Although *This Present Darkness* was not intended to be a theological treatise on the ministry of angels, it certainly piqued my curiosity on the subject. I began to realize how often I read passages in the Bible where angels are active and breeze right over them without giving much thought to what role they might play in my life.

Think about the predominance of angelic activity in the early chapters of the gospels and also in passages like Peter's release from prison in the book of Acts. Since one of the YHWH names of God is "Lord of Hosts," I have simply started to pray that God would send forth and activate those angels he has appointed to minister to my family. I pray that the host of heaven would be part of the spiritual defense system of our lives.

When I have finished this component of prayer, I find that I am able to face the day with a sense of confidence and peace. Through prayer, I have responsibly exercised the authority with which I have been entrusted to appropriate divine protection. It might be a jungle out there, but Jesus Christ is Lord, even of the "jungle"! He is able to provide spiritual protection.

When I have finished praying through this component, I have prayed through all of my "us" issues. I am now ready to turn my focus once again toward God and his agenda and address the final issues of the Lord's Prayer.

Carefully work through this chapter's assignment and begin to erect God's spiritual fortress around your life and your family.

ASSIGNMENT SEVEN:

1. Go to the section of your prayer notebook entitled "Developing Spiritual Protection".
2. Make your "A" a section on temptation. List those areas where you are especially susceptible to temptation and failure.
3. Make a list of the qualities Paul identifies as part of your spiritual armor, (see Ephesians 6:10-20).
4. Make your "B" a section on spiritual warfare.
5. Make a list of areas where you think Satan is attacking you and your family.
6. List the resources God has given you to protect you.
7. Ask God to create a "hedge" of protection around you and your family.
8. Ask God to send his angels to help you.
9. Pray at least five days this week praying through all six components.

CHAPTER 10

Final Issues

§

The Lord reigns,

(P*SALM 93:1*)

I*N* A*L*-A*NON*'*S* B*OOK OF* D*AILY* readings, *One Day at a Time in Al-
Anon*, the reading for June 14 begins with the following question:

> *If someone were to say to me: "Here is a medicine that can change
> your whole life for the better; it will put you in a state of relaxed
> serenity; help you overcome the nagging undercurrent of guilt
> for past errors, give you new insight into yourself and your spiri-
> tual value, and let you meet life's challenges with confidence and
> courage." Would I take it?*

If you wouldn't answer that question with a "Yes," you might
need to check in at your local mental health center. Although,
in context, the question is referring to the program of Alcoholics
Anonymous and Al-Anon, it is the exact question we need to ask
ourselves about the practice of prayer. Obviously, prayer requires
more work and self-discipline than taking medicine or everyone

would be doing it. Ironically, no medicine can give you the lasting serenity, insight, or spiritual growth you receive through prayer. The work and self-discipline required in prayer are critical to the growth process. "No pain, no gain" is just as true in the prayer closet as it is in the weight room or gym.

We all know the slogan, "Just Do it!" The exhortation calls us to renounce the life of a coach potato and get some exercise. It is a call to action. In relationship to the discipline of prayer, we need to cultivate the same motto.

For most of us, this is where the breakdown comes. We must translate our desire into action. As we come to the end of our study, I can guarantee you will face this hurdle. Knowing what you now know, will you develop the discipline of a regular time of significant prayer?

Recently, a good friend of mine returned from the Cooper Clinic in Dallas, Texas. It is one of the leading clinics in the world specializing in the prevention of heart disease and cancer. While my friend was there the doctors helped him develop an exercise program designed to prolong his life and help prevent a heart attack. He told me about one of their instructions that I found extremely relevant in relationship to the subject of prayer.

My friend was not only given a program to follow, he was told that he needed to develop a habit of exercising and *using* that program. Research showed that to develop a habit, he needed to exercise at least five times a week. Studies have shown that if we set a goal of only exercising three days a week it becomes too easy to make excuses and fail to *just do it!* On the other hand, when we set a goal of five days a week we have much less of a tendency to put off our exercise. Five days a week develops a habit. It also gives us grace in the event we miss a day. If our goal is every day, and we miss a day, too often we become discouraged and quit.

I found this fascinating because that is what has proven to be true in my prayer life. My personal goal has been to practice a discipline of prayer at least five days a week. Often, five becomes seven because the habit has become so ingrained. If I miss a day, I know I need to get back on the program the next day. If I am only shooting for three days a week, I know my tendency to postpone till tomorrow what I need to do today will take over. That is why in all the assignments in this book I have instructed you to ask God to help you pray for five days each week.

The physical discipline of exercising five days a week will strengthen your heart and prolong the length of your life. But the spiritual discipline of prayer will actually change your heart and transform the quality of your life.

A Little Help From our Friends

In my own life, I have observed a subtle tendency to let disciplines slide. After years of highly disciplined physical training, I began to miss workouts regularly until I simply stopped staying in shape. When I could no longer fit into my trousers, and my chest muscles sank to my waist, I decided to get back on the program.

The same tendency holds true for spiritual discipline. How can we overcome this tendency? One extremely helpful tool is to have a friend hold you accountable. Accountability is a powerful dynamic of effective change. I once taught this material to a large group of men at my church. The larger group committed to work on their prayer lives. To help make that happen, I had each man find a partner in the group and write down their phone number right on their prayer outline. Then we all committed to calling our partner regularly to remind each other about our commitment and see how each of us was doing. It sounds simple, but it is tremendously helpful. I would encourage you to do the same.

The Perfect Pattern

Using the analogy of a physical workout once again, many people never get into shape because they don't know *what* to do or *how* to get going. For many, a simple program that is easy to understand makes the difference between getting healthy or staying unfit. Learning how to start slow and build gradually plays a critical role in finally getting into shape.

In the practice of prayer, those same dynamics work. Many men and women respond to emotional appeals to pray more, but don't know where to start. They set unrealistic goals for themselves and then grow discouraged when they fail to keep those goals. It is my hope that this book is a help in overcoming both of these difficulties. If you simply follow the weekly assignments, you will begin with realistic objectives and gradually build over a period of weeks a deep and significant prayer life. I have received emails and letters from men and women around the country that have let me know it works!

Looking back over the strategy we have worked to develop; I hope you can see that Jesus gave us the perfect pattern for prayer. With your outline in hand you have a tool much like the checklist a pilot uses before takeoff.

Component One: Am I Properly Positioned to Pray?

We begin our time of prayer by focusing on our relationship with the living God. This is a time of consciously entering his presence as we remember and reflect on the truth that he is "Abba," our heavenly father, through our relationship with Jesus Christ. We enter his presence with a sense of powerlessness as we call on the Holy Spirit to help us pray as he promised he would. *Check!*

As we enter his presence, we ask for this time of prayer to be a time of true intimacy when we are in real spiritual fellowship with God, the Father. We also focus on Jesus Christ. We reaffirm that this time of prayer will be a time of surrender to his lordship in our lives. We remember that he said that when we belong to him he calls us "friend." We pray that this time of prayer would lead us into the experience of his friendship. *Check!*

We also want to remember to thank God that in our powerlessness, and the unmanageability of our lives created by that powerlessness, he is here to bring sanity, serenity, power and fruitfulness to our day. *Check!*

COMPONENT TWO: WHERE IS MY FOCUS?
Having spent adequate time praying about our relationship with God, we then begin to set our focus on him in a time of prayerful worship. We use God's names to remind us of all the wonderful dimensions of who he is. We set our hearts and minds on God's agenda. In praise and thanksgiving, we contemplate and reflect on who he is. We "enter his gates with thanksgiving and his courts with praise." *Check!*

COMPONENT THREE: WHERE DO I NEED DIVINE INTERVENTION?
In light of who God is, and as a response to our time of worship and praise, we joyfully submit to his will for our lives. We then

ask the Lord to intervene in the affairs of our day. We spend time appropriating God's divine intervention. Recognizing that God delights in our desire to have him intervene in earthly situations, we now ask him to bring the power of his kingdom to bear on:

1. Our lives – *Check!*
2. Our families – *Check!*
3. Our churches – *Check!*
4. Our cities – *Check!*
5. Our nation – *Check!*
6. Our world – *Check!*

COMPONENT FOUR: WHAT ARE MY NEEDS TODAY?
Having adequately prayed about God's agenda, and spent time focusing our attention on him, we now pray about our specific needs. We ask God, who is *Jehovah-jireh*, to provide for our daily needs.

1. We ask for our physical needs to be met – *Check!*
2. We ask for out emotional needs to be met – *Check!*
3. We ask for our spiritual needs to be met – *Check!*

We then pray about those issues and events of the day that constitute our "daily bread." *Check!*

Recognizing that many of our anxieties in life are related to wants rather than needs, we pray about all those issues that are causing anxiety in our lives. *Check!*

Finally, we pray that we would learn to live in God's kingdom provision with contentment, and that we would meet all the conditions attached to that provision. *Check!*

COMPONENT FIVE: *WHERE HAVE I FAILED?*

We next spend some time tapping into the provision of forgiveness and spiritual cleansing available through Christ's death. We acknowledge before our heavenly father that we are all spiritually defective, in constant need of his mercy and grace. *Check!*

We give thanks that Jesus' death on the cross provided full and free forgiveness for our moral, ethical, and spiritual failure. We quietly ask the Holy Spirit to reveal to us any actions, attitudes, or thoughts that need to be confessed. *Check!*

We gratefully receive the forgiveness and cleansing that God has provided. *Check!*

Having experienced forgiveness in our own lives, we also examine whether anyone has offended us since our last time of prayer. If we are harboring any bitterness or resentment toward this person, we make a conscious decision to choose to forgive the one who has sinned against us. *Check!*

COMPONENT SIX: *HAVE I DEVELOPED SPIRITUAL PROTECTION?*

In prayer, we ask God to erect a spiritual fortress around our lives and around our families by asking for his protective presence and power. *Check!*

We ask the Lord to keep us away from temptation. *Check!*

We ask the Lord to "clothe" us in the spiritual equipment of the armor of God. *Check!*

We pray that the host of heaven would be active in their ministry to us and our families this day. *Check!*

COMPONENT SEVEN: WHAT DO I NEED TO REMEMBER TODAY?
Finally, Jesus taught the disciples to end this time of prayer by affirming to our heavenly father that "Yours is the Kingdom."

This affirmation flows freely when we have experienced the presence of God during prayer. In the midst of the craziness that surrounds us in this world there *is* a higher reality. The kingdoms of this world are fading and passing away. There is only one true and lasting kingdom. That kingdom is the Kingdom of God. God is still in control. The destiny of the planet and the destiny of our lives are in his hands. We come to the end of our time of prayer confident that we can live a kingdom lifestyle today flowing out of our relationship with God. *Check!*

We want to further affirm that "Yours is the power." We began our time of prayer by acknowledging our powerlessness. It is appropriate to end our time by acknowledging God's omnipotence. His is the power! His power enables us to face the day, living in the power of the Holy Spirit. *Check!*

Finally, we are to affirm "Yours is the glory." The first question in the Westminster Confession's shorter catechism asks, "What is the chief end of man?" To put the question in more contemporary terms we might paraphrase, "What is the purpose of life?" The answer is both simple and profound: "The chief end of man is to glorify God and enjoy him forever." All we say, all we do, all we think, and all we are today is to bring glory to God. Check!

It is a perfect pattern! Seven components given to the disciples, and to us through them, by the perfect teacher. When developed, and followed, it provides a great strategy for developing a meaningful prayer life.

Assignment Eight:

1. Review all your previous assignments.
2. Complete your prayer notebook by adding a page titled "Final Affirmations."
3. Ask the Holy Spirit to help you pray five days this week.
4. Find a friend and commit to holding each other accountable.
5. *Just do it!*

CHAPTER 11
Beyond the Basics

§

Be still, and know I am God,

(PSALM 46:10)

By the time you reach this chapter you might be saying to yourself, "No more!" I can certainly understand that. On the other hand, you might also be thinking, "Wait a minute...what about...?" Even though we have covered a great deal of material in the preceding chapters there are still many areas of prayer left undiscussed.

Think of this book as a beginning course in prayer; kind of a "Prayer 101". I am convinced that for those of us who are just getting started on the journey of prayer we have many exciting years ahead of us discovering all the facets of prayer God has made available. In Teresa of Avila's *A Life of Prayer*, she uses the image of a castle to teach about the cultivation of our inner spiritual lives. The castle is built during our times alone with God. I'm quite sure Teresa actually possessed such an inner castle. For many of us, we might think our inner life is little more than a shack! Through prayer, God will change that.

Many years ago, Robert Munger wrote a classic little booklet entitled *My Heart, Christ's Home.* It is a modern version of Teresa's concept of this inner life. Munger portrays the different areas of our inner lives as rooms in a house. He encourages his readers to meet daily with Christ in the library of their inner house and to turn over every room, closet, nook, and cranny to Christ's lordship. I would suggest that Jesus not only wants to occupy every room of our existing "house" as is, but that he also has blueprints for the addition of new "rooms." He wants to build a mansion, then a castle, then a city, then a whole inner world where he reigns. I believe his intention is for our inner world and inner life to be so rich that our preoccupation with, and love of, the material world fades.

Shortly after I began praying through the pattern in this book, I went on a cross-country motorcycle trip with a group of friends. We had been planning the trip and anticipating our adventure for nearly a year. We flew to Milwaukee, Wisconsin, the birthplace of Harley-Davidson motorcycles, where most of the men in our group picked up brand new Harleys. Several of us who already owned motorcycles shipped our bikes to Milwaukee so we could ride with the group.

We rode across Wisconsin, Minnesota, South Dakota, through the Black Hills, and out to Yellowstone National Park. Some days the weather was perfect. Other days we rode through thunderstorms and high winds. It was an adventure!

In the early part of the trip, I had an important insight. I wasn't enjoying the trip as much as I had anticipated. I tried to get a handle on why. I began to think about the other exciting adventure I had been on for the previous several months. I had been regularly "traveling" into the presence of God. I had been spending hours building my inner castle. I began to realize that the richness of this inner journey actually eclipsed the excitement of my outer journey.

Nothing we experience in the physical world will ever give us the joy of our experience in the presence of God. David said it perfectly when he wrote, "In your presence (God's) is fullness of joy," (Psalm 16:11).

Fullness of joy is what all people long for. There is only one location in the universe where it is found. That place is the presence of the Lord. There is one preeminent way to get there while we are clothed with these mortal bodies – prayer.

BEYOND THE BASICS

Once you have started to develop a more meaningful experience of prayer using the strategy contained in this book, you may wonder where to go next. There are other dimensions of prayer that are not explicitly spelled out in the Lord's Prayer. Some of these other dimensions or approaches to prayer have been extremely important in the lives of men and women of prayer throughout the ages

Over the years I have come to appreciate the great diversity of God's creative genius in making each of us unique. Our uniqueness will definitely emerge in the unfolding development of our prayer lives. Some men and women have been created and shaped with personalities that are very logical and rational. Others are more oriented toward feelings and intuition. As our spiritual lives develop, these inherent distinctions will shape our relationship with God.

For some men and women nothing brings the reality of God's presence into their experience quite like reading the Bible. All the logic circuits get filled with spiritual data and God's presence comes alive. For others, sitting quietly and contemplating the sun setting over the mountains ushers them right into the presence of the Lord. Some are more mystical in their orientation. Others are not. As our prayer lives develop, we each need to discover what dimensions of prayer are the most effective for us. The pattern developed in the preceding chapters provides a framework for some of these other expressions of prayer to be explored.

CONTEMPLATION AND MEDITATION

If you analyze the approach to prayer taken in this book you will see that it is filled with specific content and a great deal of action on our part. Within certain segments of the Christian world there are much different approaches to prayer. Some from these circles might read this book and ask where the quiet, listening part of prayer is reflected in these instructions. They might point us to the text in the Old Testament where God encourages us to, "Be still, and know that I am God," (Psalm 46:10).

Mature prayer is not intended to be a monologue. It is a real encounter with the living God who wants to communicate with us. True prayer is a *dialogue* between two people. Therefore, as we grow in our experience of prayer we must learn to listen. It is this listening dimension that is emphasized by those who practice a more contemplative type of prayer.

There are certain difficulties with finding an appropriate practice of contemplative prayer. There are those who advocate the practice and those who believe it is not an appropriate spiritual discipline for Christians. Those who are negative in their assessment see the practice as being syncretistic with eastern religions who practice meditation.

To simplify a complex subject, often the difference between Christian meditation and Eastern meditation has to do with what is in our minds as we meditate. Eastern meditation involves the emptying of the mind to achieve a meditative state. From a purely physiological perspective, the chanting of a mantra occupies the lower functions of the brain so that the logic centers are kept inoperative. The same physiological phenomena could be achieved by chanting the word "bunk" over and over just as easily as chanting a mantra that often is the name of a Hindu deity.

There is also a form of meditation that involves visualization. This practice can be as simple as visualizing a peaceful landscape, to the more dangerous practice of visualizing "spirit guides" in an attempt to gain guidance from the supernatural realm. Compare this to the biblical mandate to seek the face of God. In this case a man or woman might visualize being held in the arms of a loving God or being touched by the healing hand of Jesus. The former (the spirit guide approach) is dangerous. The latter can be very helpful.

Biblically-based contemplation and meditation seeks to *fill* the mind, not empty it. Over time, as you develop the "Getting Focused" part of your prayer strategy, you can begin to contemplate, or reflect, on the significance of each *YHWH* names of God. You can take a passage of the Bible and read it slowly and the stop and think about what you have read. Then after thinking about it for some time, you can go back and read it again and think a second time about what God is saying to you through the passage. Then repeat this process a third time. In much of the classical literature on the Christian spiritual life this is called "*lectio divina.*" The term simply means "divine reading."

As we have seen before, the Bible tells us that at times God wants us to "be still, and know he is God." This involves simply sitting in the presence of God and letting the Holy Spirit guide your thought processes. This requires some real effort in our culture where most of us have been conditioned to be on the go, and where the noise is always distracting us.

My time on Fox Island was an extended time of prayer and solitude. It was a wonderful experience of fellowship with God that incorporated both active times of prayer and journaling, and long periods of silence and reflection. It is difficult to experience an authentic encounter with God when we are in a hurry. The history of the church is filled with examples of men and women who went away into the desert or mountains to spend extended time alone with God. I would encourage you to find a time and a place where you can go for a day, or even several days, to be alone and quiet with God.

INTERCESSION

Shortly after I developed my prayer outline and began to use it in my daily times of prayer, I became aware that I still wanted to pray for many people and many issues that I had not included in my outline. Prior to using this approach to prayer, I had kept a list of the needs of others I had been asked to pray for. I found it difficult to be consistent in praying for those needs. I found that the more I utilized this new approach to prayer I become more effective in praying for people and situations that needed intercession.

There are two approaches to building a ministry of intercession. One is to incorporate these needs into our existing outline. You could create a list of people and needs to pray for during your time of seeking divine intervention. I have found it more helpful to keep a separate list in my notebook and to have times of pure intercession. My list includes friends in ministry, neighbors, extended family, and needs of people in our church. I also keep a page that I call my "miracle list."

I know and believe that God can do anything. One message of the Incarnation is the "nothing is impossible with God," (Luke 1:37). In the Old Testament book of Jeremiah, God extended an invitation: "Call to me and I will answer you and show you great and unsearchable things you do not know," (Jeremiah 33:3). This invitation was given at a time when the city of Jerusalem was under siege by the Babylonian army. Soon the city would be destroyed and the people who survived would be carried into captivity. Yet God promised that a day would come when he would bring healing, forgiveness, and restoration to Israel, (Jeremiah 33:6-9). Out of this restoration would come abundant prosperity and peace. God was going to do the impossible for Israel!

There is a New Testament parallel to this great Old Testament invitation. The Apostle Paul ends the third chapter of the book of Ephesians with a benediction that includes the following phrase: "Now to him who is able to do immeasurably more than all we ask or imagine..." (Ephesians 3:20).

I have taken these two texts and written them on the top of what I call my "miracle list." Under these texts I have written the statement: *Impossible apart from intervention by the living God!*

Under this statement I have a list of needs that appear to be completely impossible, or at least so difficult that only intervention on God's part could solve the problems or meet the needs. I know God *can* do the things I pray about. I certainly don't always know if he *will* do them. I do know that he is the God who turns hard rock into springs of water (Psalm 114:8), and who does whatever pleases him (Psalm 115:3).

I have had the joy of seeing items on my "miracle list" answered. I have also had the disappointment of God saying, "No." And I'm sure that some may not be answered until Christ returns. But I think God likes it when we ask for the impossible.

The Final Frontier

I used to love to watch the old Star Trek television series. I have enjoyed the movies even more. I love Mr. Spock and his logical approach to life. I have been tempted on more than one occasion to end a worship service by giving the Vulcan "V" sign and pronouncing "Live long, and prosper" as the benediction. It seems biblical to me! The television show began each episode with the same declaration: "Space, the final frontier." But space is not the final frontier. The final frontier is the realm of the spirit. Space is finite. One day we might actually master space. It seems improbable, given the vastness of the universe, but possible. But the realm of the spirit is infinite. It will provide an eternity of unimaginable adventure and excitement.

God has given us a map to guide us on the adventure. We call it the Bible. God himself has promised to be with us on the journey. When all is said, and done, I believe we will discover that he *is* the journey. To know him, love him, serve him, and enjoy him forever – that is what eternal life will be. At the present, we see only dimly. But, our vision can be improved. God waits daily to meet with us. He delights in our desire to draw apart from the concerns and activities of the day and speak that word he longs to hear – "Father…"

Final Assignment:

1. Develop a section in your prayer notebook entitled "Intercessory Prayer."
2. List the people and needs you will pray for on a regular basis.
3. Develop a miracle list. Write out those concerns of your life that require miraculous divine intervention.
4. In prayer this week attempt to spend time quietly meditating on the names of God, the love of God, the cross of Christ, and the work of the Holy Spirit
5. Using the resources you have developed, pray at least five days this week.

CHAPTER 12

Sweet Hour of Prayer

§

Devote yourselves to prayer,

(Colossians 4:2)

AT THIS POINT, YOU STILL may not be sure what an actual time of prayer using this strategy would look like. The following transcript reflects a time of actually using the pattern. I hesitate to include this, hoping that you won't find it in any way self-serving. I have included in each section biblical references that relate to what is being prayed for and about.

This is not intended to be a perfect example. Like you, I am in the process of learning how to pray more effectively. My prayer life has a great deal of diversity, so this is only one example of what a time of prayer might look like when you put the preceding chapters together.

As you read this prayer, feel free to change my details and requests to fit your life and circumstances. Write in the book and make note of your own needs as you read. You can then go back and use this as a template for your own notebook. I've included times so you can see the duration of each element in this specific example.

GETTING POSITIONED – 6:47 A.M.

Father…I come to you for a time of fellowship and prayer this morning. Thank you for this day. Thank you for life. Thank you that I can wake up and know you are here and you love me. Abba…Father. (reflected a few minutes on God as "Abba.")

Holy Spirit, I ask you to lead me and enable me during this time. I am powerless without you. I am powerless over the effects of my former separation from you, and I don't have the ability to pray effectively without your help. Give me focus during this time. Help it be real, enjoyable, productive, and experiential. Come and draw me into your presence. (John 15:5; Romans 8:26-27)

Father, I pray for heartfelt intimacy with you today. I pray I might know you better. Help me experience your love today. Help me love you above all else. Help me live out of our father/child relationship today. (Paused and sat for a minute) (John 16:27; 17:23; Ephesians 1:17)

Lord Jesus, I submit to your lordship today. I willingly and joyfully ask you to reign in and over my life today. I pray I might sense your friendship and brotherhood. (John 15:5; Hebrews 2:11)

Holy Spirit, I ask you to work in my life today. Fill me with your presence. Move me into your flow. Be the dominant influence over every fiber of my being. I want to fully experience you today. (Romans 8:15; Ephesians 5:18)

GETTING FOCUSED – 6:54 A.M.

Father, I praise you. I worship you this morning. I pray that with my lips and through my life, you would be honored, exalted, and glorified today. I want the praise to go to you. I long to enter your gates with thanksgiving and your courts with praise.

I praise you that you are *YHWH*. You are the God who is and who causes to be. You will be who you will be. I pray that in your sovereign power and goodness you would *be* and *cause to be* in my life today. I ask that you would draw me to follow your will. (Exodus 3:14: Psalm 69:30; Psalm 100:4)

Father, I thank you today for all you have done to rescue me from the desperate situation I was in apart from your love and grace, I am eternally grateful that you are *Ya'shua (the Lord is salvation)*. Jesus, thank you for what you did for me on the cross. I would be totally lost if it were not for you. Thank you that my salvation is finished business. You are holy; you are righteous; you are full of grace, mercy, love, and kindness. I praise you and give you thanks.

I am so grateful that one of your names is *YHWH-tsidkenu*. Thank you that you make it possible for me to be right in your eyes even though in myself and my actions I am not. You are the source of all my righteousness. Thank you for the miracle of justification through Jesus.

I thank you and praise you that you are also *YHWH-m'kaddesh*. You are "the Lord who sanctifies." I desperately need the transforming work of your Holy Spirit to be active in my life today. Make me to be more the man you created me to be. (Jeremiah 23:6; Matthew 1:21; Romans 3:23-25)

Thank you that you are *YHWH-shamma* (the Lord is present). You are here. You are Immanuel – God with us. Help me be aware of your presence today. Thank you that you will never leave me or forsake me.

Holy Spirit, I am grateful that you are in me, and with me. Make your presence known and felt today. (Pause, reflect, worship) (Ezekiel 48:35; Matthew 28:20; Hebrews 13:5)

Lord, I praise you that you are *YHWH-rohi* (the Lord is my shepherd). I have seen your guidance in my life. Thank you. You have provided for me and my family. Thank you. You restore my soul. I am so grateful for the way you take care of us. Thank you for your patience and care.

Lord Jesus, you are the Good Shepherd. You are the source of abundant life and living. Thank you for your abundance. You are the source of true security. Remind me today that the false security of money, position, power, and the rest are fading away. I praise and worship you because you are a gracious, loving, and all-powerful shepherd. (*Pause and sit quietly*) (Psalm 23:1; John 10:10)

Thank you, Father, that you are *YHWH-jireh*, the source of all provision. Thank you for your providence and care for my life. Thank you that by nature and promise you are a provider. You are a good provider and a provider of good. As your Word says, no good thing do you withhold from those who walk uprightly. Every good and perfect gift comes from you. You "feed me" with the "finest of wheat."

Abba, I'm glad that your provision is rooted in your all-knowing, all-wise, all-caring, kind nature. I would ask that you would not give me anything that would not be good for me or the family. I don't want "leanness in my soul." (Genesis 22:14; Psalm 84:11; Philippians 4:19)

I praise you and thank you that you are *YHWH-rophe*, "the Lord who heals." Thank you for all the healing you have done in our lives. We desperately need your healing power at this time in our lives. I am reminded that you are the son of righteousness who has risen with healing in your wings.

Thank you for your promise of present healing. Thank you for the healing implications of your atonement. Thank you for the miracles of healing you have done in Baker's life. Thank you for healing Ali in the past and by faith thank you for what you are going to do to heal her Alzheimer's. Thank you, Father, for your lovingkindness that causes you to care about our illnesses and injuries. I praise you. (Exodus 15:26; Malachi 4:2; James 5:14-15)

Father God, I give you thanks that you are *YHWH-nissi*, "The Lord my banner." I look to you as the source of true success in my life. I thank you for your promise of a future marked by kingdom prosperity. Thank you for freedom from the failure of the curse of the Law, and the freedom of life in your Spirit. Your banner over my life is love. Because of your love and your promises, I know that no difficulty or opposition I face in life will ultimately prevail against me. I praise you! (*Pause for a time of praise.*) (Jeremiah 2911; Isaiah 54:17; Galatians 3:13-14)

Lord, you are *YHWH-shalom*, "the Lord is peace." You are the source of my well-being, wholeness, harmony, contentment, and fulfillment. Lord, fill me with your peace.

Holy Spirit, I thank you that peace is part of the fruit you produce in my life. Thank you that your promises to Abraham are fulfilled in Christ. Thank you that I live my life under your covenants. Father, nothing is more important to me today than living under your blessing. I praise you and worship you for all you are and all your name represents. Hallowed, exalted, honored, and magnified be your name! (Judges 6:24; Galatians 5:22; Ephesians 2:14)

SEEKING INTERVENTION – 7:13 A.M.

In light of all that you are, Father, and as you have taught us, I now pray that your kingdom would come, and your will would be done on earth as it is in heaven. Today, I come to ask for your divine intervention in my life and the affairs of my life. I know that I am powerless apart from you. Apart from your intervention my life is unmanageable, unproductive, frustrating, and chaotic. Apart from you, I am a mess. But I believe your power can bring sanity, power, and effectiveness to my life. I turn my will over to you today and ask that your will would be done in my life. I relinquish my agenda, and embrace yours.

I pray that your kingdom would come on my life today. I choose your lordship, depend on your empowering, and abide in you today. Make my life pleasing to you today. Help me connect with you at an experiential level today. Enable me to discern your will for me. Work in me to develop spiritual maturity and transform the defects of my character.

I pray for your blessing today, Father. I ask that you would develop my character in such a way that you can prosper and empower my life without my taking advantage of your goodness for my own ends. I ask for the kingdom realities of righteousness, peace, and joy in the Spirit to be real in my life today. Make me an object of your special favor. Let me be the apple of your eye. Love on me. Thank you, Abba. I like you a lot! (Matthew 6:9-10; John 15:5; Romans 14:17)

Holy Spirit, fill my life today. Control, empower, and guide my life. Make known to me the will of the Father and give me the grace, courage, and power to carry it out. Help me to walk in the Spirit and obey joyfully and willingly. Lead me, Lord. I'm available for your purposes. Remove any deceit from my spirit. Give me a father's heart for my family and the church. Make me an instrument of your love, your truth, and your peace. (Ephesians 4:22-24, 5:18)

I pray for Allison, Lord. She really needs your intervention. I ask for your healing power to touch her and heal her Alzheimer's. I don't know of anyone who has ever been healed of this disease, but I know you have the power to heal her. I pray your will would be done in her life today. Bless her. Prosper her. Protect her. Give her the "crown of beauty, the oil of gladness, and the garment of praise." Help me be a blessing to her today. (Isaiah 61:3)

I pray for Stephanie and Jed. Bless them, prosper them, and protect them. Bless Jaxon and Olivia. I pray you would work out your will in their lives and help them figure out how to make ends meet. Help them find a house they can afford. Help Stephanie's business begin to work. Help Stephanie figure out how to get Olivia's needs met. As the kids head back to school I pray they would have a great year and you would make sure they have the right teachers. Help them, Lord.

Thank you that Baker has been stable for over a year. I pray the changes in his medication would not make him manic. Bless him, protect him, and prosper him. Your kingdom come on his life and your will be done in his life. I pray for a neat Christian girlfriend and eventually wife. I know someone is out there that would be a good fit. Bless his music and help him become self-supporting. Thank you for his help with Allison. I believe you have orchestrated his living situation so he can help and I am grateful. Keep his kidneys from any further damage. (Psalm 63:3; 144;12)

I pray for Highline. Bless the church. Prosper it. Protect it. Keep us in the center of your will. Help our people reach out and minister to those around them. Help us know the things you want us to do. Protect us from the evil one and all his schemes to keep us ineffective.

Bless and protect the staff and elders. I pray for unity and love among the staff. Help us work out the kinks we are dealing with. Give Ken good time off and refresh him. Bless Dave and Biff as they carry the load while I'm gone. Show us who the new elders should be. Move in our congregation and bring authentic renewal in the Spirit. Bring the right people who need to be part of the church and keep the wrong people away.

Bless our President. Keep him safe. Help him make good decisions and not say so many stupid things. Bless Senator Gardner and Senator Bennet. Give them wisdom and use them to make good decisions in this critical time. Help the Republicans and Democrats quit fighting so much and begin to work together. There are millions of believers in America. Help us have a more positive impact on our nation. Keep us from self-destruction.

Frustrate the plans of North Korea. Bring pressure to bear from China. Bring peace to the planet. Restore the climate. Give wisdom about how to do that.

Praying for Provision – 7:38 a.m.

Father, give us this day our daily bread. Thank you that you are *YHWH-jireh*. You are the ultimate source of all our provision. Thank you for this day's bread. Thank you for meeting our material needs. Thank you for a good job. Help me be a faithful and responsible manager and steward of the resources you have given us. Keep me seeking your kingdom and making your will my ultimate priority. Help me be a faithful giver.

I ask for biblical prosperity. I am your servant. Your word says you delight in the prosperity of your servant. Help me meet the conditions attached to your provision. You always meet our needs.

I want to bring before you some of my desires. I ask that those things that are part of your will, you would give. I also ask that if any of these requests or desires would not be good for me, you would graciously not grant them.

Help me save enough for retirement. Help me still trust you, not what I put aside. Help me be able to pay for Ali's health care. I confess I am fearful of not being able to pay for memory care for her. Help me trust you with this.

Help me eat better and get the exercise I need. I feel stuck and out of the habit and need to get back in gear. Help me get Ali to get more exercise.

You know I am a car enthusiast. Thank you for the cars we have and the motorcycles. I like change. I don't want to make stupid decisions so work out good trades.

I am grateful for the life you have given us. You have blessed us. Thank you for our family. Thank you for our home. Thank you for your love. (Psalm 35:27; Matthew 6;33; Philippians 4:6)

Appropriating Forgiveness – 7:45 a.m.

I confess today that I am a sinner by nature and constantly in need of your grace and forgiveness. I am restless, irritable, and discontent. Work in me to replace those qualities with peace, joy, and a grateful heart. I confess my lust, greed, anger, insecurity, self-centeredness, and lack of kindness. I ask you to work by the power of the Holy Spirit to transform these defects and make me more like Jesus. I hate when I'm impatient with Allison. Search me and show me anything I need to confess. (*Paused and allowed time for the Spirit to reveal anything I needed to deal with.*)

Allow me to treat any offense against me today with forgiveness. To the best of my ability I am not aware of any bitterness or lack of forgiveness I am harboring. If I am, reveal it to me. If I have offended anyone and need to seek amends, show me. (*pause*) Thank you that you died for all this crap! Thank you for your grace and power. (Psalm 32:1-5; I John 1:9)

Praying for Protection – 7:47 a.m.

Father, lead me not into temptation today. Deliver us from all the schemes and attacks of the evil one. I ask you to keep me away from the attraction and seduction of sin today. Teach me the lessons I need to learn in some other way. Clothe me in the spiritual armor of righteousness, truthfulness, integrity, and humility.

Activate the "hedge" around our lives and our home today. Fire up the "force field" of your power and your presence. Drive out any "predators" who have infiltrated the "vineyard." Protect our lives from the destructive attacks of the enemy. Cover us with Your presence and release the host of heaven assigned to us to surround our lives today. You are my refuge and fortress. Protect me today. Protect Ali and Baker today. Help me live out of the reality of my position in you, and help me exercise the spiritual authority you have given me. (Job 1:10; Ephesians 6:12-14; Hebrews 1:14)

Affirmation – 7:49 a.m.

Lord, I affirm that yours is the kingdom, and I am immensely grateful for that fact. Help me live a kingdom lifestyle today.

I also affirm that yours is the power. In all of my powerlessness, I ask you to strengthen me with power in my inner being that I might please you today and do your will.

Yours, and yours alone, is all the glory. I ask you to transform me into your image with ever-increasing glory. May my life be pleasing and glorifying to you today.

In Jesus' Name, I pray.

NOTE: As time and leading allow, I pray through my lists of intercessory prayer needs and my miracle list. Today I prayed especially for healing for Allison.

Example of a Prayer Notebook

I. GETTING STARTED – "FATHER"

  A. Empowerment/Getting Help
    1. Intervention
    2. Enablement
    3. Focus
    4. Quality time
  B. Relationship
    3. Father – Abba
      a. Heartfelt intimacy
      b. Love
      c. Sonship
    2. Son – Jesus Christ
      a. Lordship
      b. Friendship
    3. Spirit – Holy Spirit
      a. Filling/ into the "flow"

II. GETTING FOCUSED – "HALLOWED BE YOUR NAME"

   A. The Name – YHWH
      1. I AM - Eternal
      2. I Cause to Be - Creator
      3. I Will be Who I Will Be – Sovereign
   B. The Names
      1. *YHWH-tsidken*u – "the Lord is righteousness
      2. *YHWH-m'kaddesh* – "the Lord who sanctifies
      3. *Ya'shua* – Jesus – my salvation
      4. *YHWH-shamma* – "the Lord is present"
         a. "I am with you" – *YHWH*
         b. Immanuel – "God with us"
      5. *YHWH-rohi* – "the Lord is my shepherd"
         a. My provider – green pastures
         b. My guide – paths of righteousness
         c. My protector – his rod and staff
         d. My provider – source of my security
      6. *YHWH-jireh* – "the Lord will provide"
         a. Good provider
         b. Provider of good
         c. Promise of provision
      7. *YHWH-rophe* – "the Lord who heals you"
         a. Healing "by his stripes"
         b. Gifts of healing
         c. Healing gifts
      8. *YHWH-nissi* – "the Lord is my banner"
         a. Promise of victory
         b. Source of victory – Jesus
         c. Freedom from failure
         d. "No weapon forged against you will prevail." (Is. 54:17)

9. *YHWH-shalom* – "the Lord is peace"
   a. Peace of God – wholeness, harmony, well- being, contentment, satisfaction, blessing
   b. Source of peace – Jesus
   c. Covenants of God – salvation, sonship, blessing, provision, prosperity
C. Thanksgiving and praise:
   1. His character – holy, righteous, just, infinite, eternal, omnipotent, omnipresent, omniscient, sovereign, wise
   2. His heart – loving, merciful, gracious, kind, caring, good

III. GETTING INTERVENTION – "YOUR KINGDOM COME"

   A. In my life (*What do you want?*)
      1. Your blessing
      2. Intimacy with you
      3. Walk in the Spirit (stay in the flow)
      4. Experience the Kingdom: righteousness, peace, joy, health, prosperity, identity
   B. In my family – your blessing, prosperity, and protection
      1. Allison
         a. Healing
         b. Joy
         c. Help
      2. Baker
         a. Stability
         b.   Friends
         c. Spiritual life
         d. Wife
      3. Stephanie and Jed
         a. Marriage
         b. Financial needs
         c. Health
         d. Olivia
         e. Jaxon
   C. In the Church – blessing, prosperity, and protection
      1. Staff: Ken, Biff, Dave, Tyler, Lori, Jennifer, Jon
      2. Elders: Bob, Buzz, Gene, Jim, Mike, Lee
      3. Vision and direction
      4. Pleasing to you
      5. Renewal and revival
      6. Impact the city

D. In the Nation
   1. The President
   2. Our Senators
   3. Our Congressman
   4. Revival and reformation
   5. Return to greatness and goodness
E. In the World
   1. Peace
   2. Stop North Korea
   3. Persecuted Church
   4. Spread of the Gospel

IV. GETTING PROVISION – "GIVE US THIS DAY…"

A. Our needs
  1. Financial provision
  2. Kingdom prosperity and success
  3. Meeting the conditions of provision
  4. Daily tasks
  5. Rest and renewal
  6. Friends
  7. Fellowship
B. My desires
  1. Car and motorcycle
  2. Vacation
  3. Clothes
  4. Books written and published
  5. Work on films and TV
C. Sources of anxiety
  1. Ali's health
  2. Baker's health
  3. My health
  4. Retirement

V. EXPERIENCING FORGIVENESS – "FORGIVE US OUR SINS"

A. Confession
1. *Lord, I am a sinner, constantly in need of your grace and forgiveness.*
2. *Lord Jesus Christ, son of God, have mercy on me, a sinner.*
3. Character defects transformed:
    a. Restless
    b. Irritable
    c. Discontent
4. Old nature: lust, greed, rage, meanness, self-centered, harsh, insecure, envy
5. *Search me, Holy Spirit.*
B. Forgiveness
1. Those who have offended.
2. Bitterness

VI. PRAYING FOR PROTECTION – "DELIVER US FROM EVIL"

A. Avoid temptation
    1. Personal holiness
    2. Armor of God
    3. Biblical humility
    4. Spiritual authority
B. Deliver from the Evil One
    1. Spiritual "hedge"
    2. Refuge and fortress
    3. Presence and power
    4. Host of heaven

VII. FINAL AFFIRMATIONS - "YOURS IS..."

A. The Kingdom – *Let me live kingdom life today.*
B. The Power – *Strengthen me with power today.*
C. The Glory – *Glorify yourself through me today.*

Developing a Prayer Notebook

§

I. GETTING STARTED – "FATHER"

II. GETTING FOCUSED – "HALLOWED BE YOUR NAME"

III. GETTING INTERVENTION – "YOUR KINGDOM COME"

IV. GETTING PROVISION – "GIVE US THIS DAY"

V. EXPERIENCING FORGIVENESS – "FORGIVE US OUR SINS"

VI. PRAYING FOR PROTECTION – "DELIVER US FROM EVIL"

VII. FINAL AFFIRMATIONS – "YOUR IS ..."

Author

§

BOB BELTZ IS A MINISTER, teacher, author and film producer. He earned his B.A from the University of Missouri, and his M.A. and Doctor of Ministry degrees from Denver Seminary.

Bob was co-founder and Teaching Pastor of Cherry Hills Community Church in Highlands Ranch, Colorado and Senior Pastor of High Street Community Church in Santa Cruz, California.

Bob serves as a special advisor to Philip Anschutz, Chairman of the Board of The Anschutz Corporation. In this role Bob helped develop, produce, and market films for the Anschutz Film Group, parent company of Walden Media (*The Lion, the Witch, and the Wardrobe, Prince Caspian, The Voyage of the Dawn Treader, Amazing Grace, Because of Winn-Dixie*) and Bristol Bay Productions (*Ray, Sahara*). Bob was the co-producer of Crusader Entertainment's film *Joshua*, He was an Associate Producer of the Emmy nominated *The Bible Series* on the History Channel, *A.D.: The Bible Continues* on NBC, and the movie *Son of God*.

Bob is the author of fifteen books, including the novels *Somewhere Fast*, a story about God, Harley-Davidsons, Route 66, and the spiritual journey; *She Loves You*, a coming of age story set in Kansas City in 1968, and *Lilith Redeemed*, based on the George McDonald classic, *Lilith*. He is the author of *Real Christianity*, an update of William Wilberforce's classic work. As the President of The Telos Project ministry, Bob continues to write, teach, and speak both nationally and internationally for both Christian and secular groups. He has been a featured speaker at the International Convention of the YMCA, Promise Keepers, the Council on National Policy, the CEO Forum at the Aspen Institute, and the Steamboat Institute.

Bob is currently the Senior Pastor of Highline Community Church in Greenwood Village, Colorado.

Made in the USA
Coppell, TX
18 May 2020